Ability is what you're capable of doing.
Motivation determines what you do.
Attitude determines how well you do it.

LOU HOLTZ
Former Notre Dame Football Coach

HOW
HIGH
WILL YOU
CLIMB?

DETERMINE YOUR SUCCESS BY
CULTIVATING THE RIGHT ATTITUDE

John C. Maxwell

NELSON
BOOKS

An Imprint of Thomas Nelson

Published in Nashville, Tennessee, by Nelson Books, an imprint of Thomas Nelson. Nelson Books and Thomas Nelson are registered trademarks of HarperCollins Christian Publishing, Inc.

Published in association with literary agency Yates & Yates, 1100 Town & Country Road, Suite 1300, Orange, California.

Thomas Nelson titles may be purchased in bulk for educational, business, fund-raising, or sales promotional use. For information, please e-mail SpecialMarkets@ ThomasNelson.com.

Unless otherwise noted, Scripture quotations are taken from the NEW AMERICAN STANDARD BIBLE®, © Lockman Foundarion 1960, 1962, 1963, 1968, 1971, 1972, 1973, 1975, 1977, 1995. Used by permission.

Scripture quotations marked TLB are taken from *The Living Bible.* © 1971. Used by permission of Tyndale House Publishers, Inc., Wheaton, Illinois 60189. All rights reserved.

How High Will You Climb? is an abridgment of *The Winning Attitude*, originally published in 1993.

Library of Congress Cataloging-in-Publication Data

Maxwell, John C., 1947–
  [Your attitude]
  How high will you climb? : determine your success by cultivating the right attitude / John C. Maxwell.
     pages cm
  Originally published as: Your attitude. San Bernardino, Calif. : Here's Life Publishers, c1984.
  Includes bibliographical references.
  ISBN 978-1-4002-0591-2
1. Attitude (Psychology)—Religious aspects—Christianity. 2. Christian life.
3. Success—Religious aspects—Christianity. I. Title.
  BV4509.5.M34 2014   248.4—dc23
               Printed in the United States of America

               14 15 16 17 18 RRD 6 5 4 3 2 1

How High Will You Climb? *is dedicated to*
Dr. Tom Phillippe, Sr.
He is my friend, a co-laborer in the gospel, and
an example of proper attitude living.

Contents

Acknowledgments

Thanks for this book must be expressed to my parents, Melvin and Laura Maxwell, for providing a home life that was accented with healthy attitudes for living. Positive attitudes, which are more caught than taught, surrounded me from the day I was born.

My wife, Margaret, provided wise counsel, and our children, Elizabeth and Joel Porter, gave me many illustrations. The Maxwell family is trying to live the principles of this book.

Appreciation is also to be given to my former staff at Skyline Wesleyan Church for their input into this book. Their insights, questions, and suggestions highlighted many Tuesday staff meetings. Barbara Brumagin, my administrative assistant at the time, especially followed through on this project.

Thank you to Paul Nanney for his friendship and exciting flying experiences that added to this book.

SECTION I

THE CONSIDERATION
OF YOUR ATTITUDE

1

It's a Bird . . .
It's a Plane . . .
No, It's an Attitude!

.

It was a beautiful day in San Diego, and my friend Paul wanted to take me for a ride in his airplane. Being new to Southern California, I decided to see our home territory from a different perspective. We sat in the cockpit as Paul completed his instrument checks. Everything was A-Okay, so Paul revved the engines and we headed down the runway. As the plane lifted off, I noticed the nose was higher than the rest of the airplane. I also noticed that while the countryside was truly magnificent, Paul continually watched the instrument panel.

Since I am not a pilot, I decided to turn the pleasure ride into a learning experience. "All those gadgets," I began, "what do they tell you? I notice you keep looking at that one instrument more than the others. What is it?"

"That's the attitude indicator," he replied.

"How can a plane have an attitude?"

"In flying, the attitude of the airplane is what we call the position of the aircraft in relation to the horizon."

By now my curiosity had been aroused, so I asked him to explain more. "When the airplane is climbing," he said, "it has a nose-high attitude because the nose of the airplane is pointed above the horizon."

"So," I jumped in, "when the aircraft is diving, you would call that a nose-down attitude."

"That's right," my instructor continued. "Pilots are concerned about attitude of the airplane because that indicates its performance."

He demonstrated by bringing the aircraft into a nose-high attitude. Sure enough, the plane began to climb, and speed decreased. He changed the attitude, and that changed the performance.

Paul concluded the lesson by saying, "Since the attitude of the airplane determines its performance, instructors now teach 'attitude flying.'"

That conversation triggered my thinking concerning people's attitudes. Doesn't an individual's attitude dictate his performance? Does she have an "attitude indicator" that continually evaluates her perspective and achievements in life? What happens when the attitude is dictating undesirable results? How can the attitude be changed? And, if the attitude changes, what are the ramifications to other people around him?

My friend Paul had an instructor's manual on "Attitude Flying," the relationship between the aircraft's attitude and its performance. We, too, have been given a handbook to attitude living—the Bible.

The apostle Paul, when writing to the church at Philippi, placed before those Christians an attitude indicator. "Have this attitude in yourselves which was also in Christ Jesus" (Phil. 2:5).

Christ gives us a perfect example to follow. His high standard was not given to frustrate us but to reveal areas in our lives that need improvement. Whenever I study Philippians 2:3–8, I am reminded of the healthy attitude qualities that Jesus possessed.

He was selfless. "Do nothing from selfishness or empty conceit, but with humility of mind let each of you regard one another as more important than himself; do not merely look out for your own personal interests, but also for the interests of others" (vv. 3–4).

He was secure. "Who, although He existed in the form of God, did not regard equality with God a thing to be grasped, but emptied Himself, taking the form of a bondservant, and being made in the likeness of men" (vv. 6–7).

He was submissive. "And being found in appearance as a man, He humbled Himself by becoming obedient to the point of death, even death on a cross" (v. 8).

Paul says that these qualities were exhibited in the life of Christ because of His attitude (v. 5). He also says that we can have this same attitude in our lives. We have a visual example of a Christian attitude, and we are encouraged to attain it.

Paul states in Romans 12:1–2:

Therefore I urge you, brethren, by the mercies of God, to present your bodies a living and holy sacrifice, acceptable to God, *which is* your spiritual service of worship. And do not be conformed to this world, but be transformed [How?] by the *renewing of your mind*, that you may prove what the will of God is, that which is good and acceptable and perfect. (emphasis mine)

The result of a renewed mind or a changed attitude is to prove and fulfill God's will. Again we see that the attitude dictates performance. I once preached a message from Psalm 34 entitled "How to Face Fear." David was lonely, fearful, and frustrated in a cave surrounded by the enemy when he wrote this comforting message. The opening of the chapter enables the reader to see the reason for David's success even when surrounded by problems.

David's Three-Fold Process of Praise

1. Praise begins with the will (v. 1).

     "I will bless the Lord at all times; His praise shall continually be in my mouth." David's attitude reflects a determination to rejoice regardless of the situation.

2. Praise flows to the emotion (v. 2).

     "My soul shall make its boast in the Lord." Now David is praising the Lord not only because it's right but also because he feels like it.

3. Praise spreads to others (vv. 2-3).

     "The humble shall hear and rejoice. O magnify the Lord with me, and let us exalt His name together." David demonstrates that the desired performance—praise—begins with an attitude that is determined to do it. The conclusion of the chapter records David's triumph. "The Lord redeems the soul of His servants, and none of these who take refuge in Him will be condemned."

Attitude living, like attitude flying, says "my attitude dictates my performance." That canopy represents a lot of ground to cover in one book. We'll need to examine:

- What is an attitude, and why is it important?
- What are the necessary ingredients for a high-performance attitude?
- What causes an attitude to become negative? Disappointing?
- How can a wrong attitude that is working against us be turned around to work for us?

Along the way we will discover the attitude indicators revealed in persons described in the Bible, the best handbook on attitude performance available since God Himself gave it to us. Obviously, this book will not be the last word on this critical subject. But I hope it will be an enlightening word to those who understand the importance of attitude. I pray it will be helpful to those who want to change.

———— Attitude Application ————

Take a few minutes before proceeding, and ask yourself the following questions:

Have I checked my attitude lately?

How would I rate my attitude?

Never been better	☐	Nose-high	☐
Never been worse	☐	Nose-down	☐

What is an attitude indicator (something that reflects my perspective) in my life?

2

The Attitude—What Is It?

The high school basketball team I played for was not having a good season, and one day the coach had one of those team meetings in which every player was quiet and listening. The coach continually stressed the relationship between the team's attitude and the win-loss record. I can still hear his words: "Fellows, your abilities say 'win,' but your attitudes say 'lose.'"

Parents are called to school for a conference regarding their child. The issue? Timmy, a fifth grader, has failing grades and is causing a disturbance among his classmates. His aptitude tests show he is intellectually capable, yet he is failing miserably. The teacher suggests he has a "bad attitude."

A member of the congregation is being discussed in a

pastoral staff meeting. Constantly recurring in the conversation is the phrase "She has a terrific attitude."

Hardly a day goes by without the word *attitude* entering a conversation. It may be used as a complaint or a compliment. It could mean the difference between a promotion or a demotion. Sometimes we sense it; other times we see it. Yet it is difficult to explain.

The attitude is an inward feeling expressed by behavior. That is why an attitude can be seen without a word being said. Haven't we all noticed the pout of the sulker or the jutted jaw of the determined? Of all the things we wear, our expressions are the most important.

The Bible teaches us that "God sees not as a man sees, for man looks at the outward appearance, but the LORD looks at the heart" (1 Sam. 16:7). "The heart is more deceitful than all else and is desperately sick; who can understand it?" (Jer. 17:9). These statements express our inability to know for sure what emotions are going on inside someone else. Yet while we refrain from judging others by their outward expressions, many times the outward actions become a "window to the soul." A person who gives "a look that kills" probably is not inwardly singing, "Something Good Is Going to Happen to You."

Acts 20 gives the account of Paul stopping at Miletus and calling for the Ephesian elders. These men gathered and listened to Paul's farewell address. The future was uncertain and their leader declared, "And now, behold, bound in spirit, I am on my way to Jerusalem, not knowing what will happen to me there, except that the Holy Spirit solemnly testifies to me in every city, saying that bonds and afflictions await me" (vv. 22–23).

Paul exhorted these church leaders to watch over the work that he had begun. Inwardly they were moved with compassion for the man who had discipled them. Their attitudes of love resulted in a touching display of affection. "And when he had said these things, he knelt down and prayed with them all. And they began to weep aloud and embraced Paul, and repeatedly kissed him, grieving especially over the word which he had spoken, that they should see his face no more. And they were accompanying him to the ship" (vv. 36–38).

Since an attitude often is expressed by our body language and by the looks on our faces, it can be contagious. Have you noticed what happens to a group of people when one person, by his expression, reveals a negative attitude? Or have you noticed the lift you receive when a friend's facial expression shows love and acceptance?

David's music and presence encouraged a troubled King Saul. Scripture tells us "the spirit of the LORD departed from Saul, and an evil spirit from the LORD terrorized him" (1 Sam. 16:14). The king's men were told to find someone who could lift their ruler's spirit. They brought David into the palace and "Saul loved him greatly. . . . And Saul sent to Jesse, saying, 'Let David now stand before me; for he has found favor in my sight.' So it came about whenever the evil spirit from God came to Saul, David would take the harp and play it with his hand; and Saul would be refreshed and be well, and the evil spirit would depart from him" (vv. 21–23).

Sometimes the attitude can be masked outwardly, and others who see us are fooled. But usually the cover-ups will not last long. There is that constant struggle as the attitude tries to wiggle its way out.

My father enjoys telling the story of the four-year-old who had one of those trouble-filled days. After reprimanding him, his mother finally said to him, "Son, you go over to that chair and sit on it now!" The little lad went to the chair, sat down, and said, "Mommy, I'm sitting on the outside, but I'm standing up on the inside."

Have you ever said that to God? We have all experienced the inner conflict similar to the one expressed by Paul in Romans 7:

> For the good that I wish, I do not do; but I practice the very evil that I do not wish . . . but I see a different law in the members of my body, waging war against the law of my mind, and making me a prisoner of the law of sin which is in my members. Wretched man that I am! Who will set me free from the body of this death? Thanks be to God through Jesus Christ our Lord! So then, on the one hand I myself with my mind am serving the law of God, but on the other, with my flesh the law of sin. (vv. 19, 23–25)

Sound familiar? Whenever a sincere Christian asks me to help him with his spiritual walk, I always talk about obedience. The simplicity of "Trust and Obey," that great hymn by John H. Sammis, points to the importance of our obedient attitude to our spiritual growth.

> When we walk with the Lord in the light of His Word
> What a glory He sheds on our way!
> While we do His good will, He abides with us still,
> And with all who will trust and obey.
> Trust and obey, for there's no other way,
> to be happy in Jesus, but to trust and obey.[1]

During a time of congregational renewal at Skyline Wesleyan Church, where I am the senior pastor, my heart was challenged with the words of Mary, the mother of Jesus, who said, "Whatever He [Jesus] says to you, do it." I shared with my congregation this thought of obedience drawn from the story of Jesus' miracle at the wedding in Cana (John 2:1–8).

Whatever Jesus says to you, do it, even though:

1. You are not in the "right place" (v. 2).

   They were at a wedding and not a church when Jesus performed the miracle. Some of God's greatest blessings will be at "other places" if we will be obedient to Him.

2. You have a lot of problems (v. 3).

   They had run out of wine. Too many times our problems drive us away from Jesus instead of to Him. Christian renewal begins when we focus on God's power and not our problems.

3. You are not encouraged (v. 4).

   Jesus said to those at the wedding, "My hour has not yet come." Instead of being discouraged by these words, Mary laid hold of the possibility of a miracle.

4. You have not walked with Him very long (v. 5).

   The servants who obeyed Jesus had just met Him, and the disciples had just started following the Lord, yet they were expected to obey Him.

5. You have not seen Him work miracles in your life.

   This was our Lord's first miracle. The people in this situation had to obey Him without His having a previous track record.

6. You don't understand the entire process.

   From this biblical story we can draw out a definition for obedience. It is listening to the words of Jesus and doing His will. Inward obedience provides outward growth.

Psychologist and philosopher James Allen states, "You cannot travel within and stand still without."[2] Soon, what is happening within us will affect what is happening without. A hardened attitude is a dreaded disease. It causes a closed mind and a dark future. When the attitude is positive and conducive to growth, the mind expands, and the progress begins.

What is an attitude?

It is the "advance man" of our true selves.
Its roots are inward but its fruit is outward.
It is our best friend and our worst enemy.
It is more honest and more consistent than our words.
It is an outward look based on past experiences.
It is a thing that draws people to us or repels them.
It is never content until it is expressed.
It is the librarian of our past.
It is the speaker of our present.
It is the prophet of our future.

——— Attitude Application ———

Choose a friend and evaluate his attitude. Write down several words that describe it. What is his performance indicator as a result of that attitude? Now do this for yourself.

3

The Attitude—Why
Is It Important?

We live in a world of words. Attached to these words are meanings that bring varied responses from us. Words such as *happiness*, *acceptance*, *peace*, and *success* describe what each of us desires. But there is one word that will either heighten the possibility of our desires being fulfilled or prevent them from becoming a reality within us.

While leading a conference in South Carolina, I tried the following experiment. To reveal the significance of this word, I read the previous paragraph and asked, "What word describes what will determine our happiness, acceptance, peace, and success?" The audience began to express words such as *job*, *education*, *money*, and *time*. Finally someone said *attitude*. Such an important area of our lives was a second thought. Our attitude is the primary force that will determine whether we succeed or fail.

For some, attitude presents a difficulty in every opportunity; for others it presents an opportunity in every difficulty. Some climb with a positive attitude, while others fall with a negative perspective. The very fact that the attitude "makes some" while "breaking others" is significant enough for us to explore its importance. Studying the major statements listed in this chapter will highlight this truth to us.

Attitude Axiom #1:
Our attitude determines our approach to life.

The story of the two buckets underlines this truth. One bucket was an optimist, and the other was a pessimist.

"There has never been a life as disappointing as mine," said the empty bucket as it approached the well. "I never come away from the well full but what I return again empty."

"There has never been such a happy life as mine," said the full bucket as it left the well. "I never come to the well empty but what I go away again full."

Our attitude tells us what we expect from life. If our "noses" are pointed up, we are taking off; if they are pointed down, we may be headed for a crash.

One of the valid ways to test your attitude is to answer this question: Do you feel your world is treating you well? If your attitude toward the world is excellent, you will receive excellent results. If you feel so-so about the world, your response from the world will be average. Feel badly about your world, and you will seem to have only negative feedback from life. Look around you. Analyze the conversations of people who lead unhappy, unfulfilled lives. You will find they are crying out against a society that they feel is out to get them and to give them a lifetime of trouble, misery, and bad luck. Sometimes the prison of discontent has been built by their own hands.

The world doesn't care whether we free ourselves from this prison or not. It marches on. Adopting a good, healthy attitude toward life does not affect society nearly so much as it affects us. The change cannot come from others. It must come from us.

The apostle Paul had a terrible background to overcome. He told Timothy that he was the "chief of sinners" (1 Tim. 1:15). But after his conversion he was infused with a desire to know Christ in a greater way. How did he fulfill this desire? Not by waiting for someone else to assist him. Neither did he look backward and whine about his terrible past. Paul diligently "pressed on to lay hold of Jesus" (Phil. 3:12). His singleness of purpose caused him to state, "But one thing I do: forgetting what lies behind and reaching forward to what lies ahead, I press on toward the goal for the prize of the upward call of God in Christ Jesus" (Phil. 3:13–14).

We are individually responsible for our view of life. The Bible says, "Whatever a man sows, this he will also reap" (Gal. 6:7). Our attitude and action toward life help determine what happens to us.

It is impossible for us to tailor-make all situations to fit our lives perfectly. But it is possible to tailor-make our attitudes to fit. The apostle Paul beautifully demonstrated this truth while he was imprisoned in Rome. He certainly had not received a "fair shake." The atmosphere of his confinement was dark and cold. Yet he writes to the church at Philippi brightly declaring, "Rejoice in the Lord *always*; again I will say, rejoice!" (Phil. 4:4, emphasis mine). Was Paul losing his mind? No. The secret is found late in the same chapter. Paul states:

Not that I speak from want; for I have *learned* to be content in whatever circumstances I am. I know how to get along with humble means and I also know how to live in prosperity; in any and every circumstance I have *learned* the secret of being filled and going hungry, both of having abundance and suffering need (vv. 11–12, emphasis mine).

The ability to tailor-make his attitude to his situation in life was learned behavior. It did not come automatically. The behavior was learned, and a positive outlook became natural. Paul repeatedly teaches us by his life that man helps create his environment—mental, emotional, physical, and spiritual—by the attitude he develops.

———— Attitude Application ————

Circle the number that most closely reveals your attitude toward life:

1. "Make the World Go Away"
2. "Raindrops Keep Falling on My Head"
3. "I Did It My Way"   .
4. "Oh What a Beautiful Morning"

ATTITUDE AXIOM #2:
OUR ATTITUDE DETERMINES OUR
RELATIONSHIPS WITH PEOPLE.

The Golden Rule: "Therefore, however you want people to treat you, so treat them" (Matt. 7:12).

This axiom takes on a higher significance when, as Christians, we realize that effective ministry to one another is based on relationships.

The model of ministry is best captured in John 13. Christ and His disciples are gathered in the upper room.

The components of Christ's model of ministry are

1. individuals with whom He had shared all areas of life,
2. an attitude and demonstration of servanthood, and
3. an all-encompassing command of relational love ("By this all men will know you are My disciples" [John 13:35]).

An effective ministry of relating to others must include all three of these biblical components. No single methodology (preaching, counseling, visitation) will effectively minister to all the needs all the time. It takes a wise combination of many methods to reach the needs of people. And the bridge between the gospel remedy and people's needs is leadership based on relationship.

John 10:3–5 gives a view of relational leadership:

1. Relationship to the point of instant *recognition* (He calls His own sheep by name);
2. Established relationship built on *trust* (His sheep hear His voice and come to Him);
3. *Modeled* leadership (He walks ahead of them, and they follow Him).

Yet establishing such relationships is difficult. People are funny. They want a place in the front of the bus, the back of the church, and the middle of the road. Tell a man there are 300 billion stars, and he will believe you. Tell him that a bench has just been painted, and he has to touch it to be sure.

The Stanford Research Institute (www.sri.com) says that the money you make in any endeavor is determined only 12.5 percent by knowledge and 87.5 percent by your ability to deal with people.

That is why Teddy Roosevelt said, "The most important single ingredient to the formula of success is knowing how to get along with people."

When the attitude we possess places others first, and we see people as important, then our perspective will reflect their viewpoint, not ours. Until we walk in the other person's shoes and see life through another's eyes, we will be like the man who angrily jumped out of his car after a collision with another car. "Why don't you people watch where you're driving?" he shouted wildly. "You're the fourth car I've hit today!"

Years ago, I was traveling in the South and stopped at a service station for some fuel. It was a rainy day, yet the station workers were diligently trying to take care of the customers. I was impressed by the first-class treatment and fully understood the reason when I read this sign on the front door of the station:

Why Customers Quit

> 1 percent die
> 3 percent move away
> 5 percent other friendships
> 9 percent competitive reasons (price)
> 14 percent product dissatisfaction
> BUT . . .
> 68 percent quit because of an attitude of indifference
> toward them by some employee!

In other words, 68 percent quit because the workers did not have a customer mind-set working for them.

Usually the person who rises within an organization has a good attitude. The promotions did not give that individual an outstanding attitude, but an outstanding attitude resulted in promotions. A study by Telemetrics International pertained to those "nice guys" who had climbed the corporate ladder. A total of 16,000 executives were studied. Observe the difference between executives defined as "high achievers" (those who generally have a healthy attitude) and "low achievers" (those who generally have an unhealthy attitude):

High achievers tended to care about people as well as profits; low achievers were preoccupied with their own security.

High achievers viewed subordinates optimistically; low achievers showed a basic distrust of subordinates' abilities.

High achievers sought advice from their subordinates; low achievers didn't.

High achievers were listeners; low achievers avoided communication and relied on policy manuals.

—— Attitude Application ——

Challenge: For one week treat every person you meet, without a single exception, as the most important person on earth. You will find that they will begin treating you the same way.

ATTITUDE AXIOM #3:
OFTEN OUR ATTITUDE IS THE ONLY DIFFERENCE BETWEEN SUCCESS AND FAILURE.

History's greatest achievements have been made by people who excelled only slightly over the masses of others in their fields. This could be called the principle of the slight edge. Many times that slight edge was attitude.

A Princeton seminary professor discovered that the spirit of optimism really does make a difference. He made a study of great preachers across past centuries. He noted their tremendous varieties of personalities and gifts. Then he asked the question, "What do the outstanding pulpiteers all have in common besides their faith?" After several years of searching, he found the answer. It was their cheerfulness. In most cases they were happy men.

Attitude Application

There is very little difference between people, but that little difference makes a big difference. That difference is attitude. Think of something that you desire. What attitude will you need to get it or achieve it?

Attitude Axiom #4:
Our attitude at the beginning of a task will affect its outcome more than anything else.

Coaches understand the importance of their teams having the right attitude before facing a tough opponent. Surgeons want to see their patients mentally prepared before going into surgery. Job-seekers know that their prospective employers are looking for more than just skills when they apply for work. Why? Because the right attitude in the beginning ensures success at the end. You are acquainted with the saying "All's well that ends well." An equal truth is "All's well that begins well."

One of the key principles I taught when leading evangelism conferences was the importance of our attitude when witnessing to others. Many times it is the way we present the gospel rather than the gospel itself that offends people. Two people can share the same news with the same person and receive different results. Why? Usually the difference is the attitude of the person sharing. The eager witness says to himself, "People are hungry for the gospel and desirous of a positive change in their lives."

The reluctant witness says to himself, "People are not interested in spiritual things and don't want to be bothered." These two attitudes will not only determine the number of attempts made in witnessing (can you guess which one will witness more often?) but also the results if they both share the same faith.

Most projects fail or succeed before they begin.

A young mountain climber and an experienced guide were ascending a high peak in the Sierras. Early one morning the young climber was suddenly awakened by a tremendous cracking sound.

He was convinced that the end of the world had come. The guide responded, "It's not the end of the world, just the dawning of a new day." As the sun rose, it was merely hitting the ice and causing it to melt.

Many times we have been guilty of viewing our future challenges as the sunset of life rather than the sunrise of a bright, new opportunity.

———— Attitude Application ————

Why not write down a project that you have neglected because of an unhealthy attitude toward it? Read axiom #4 again and again, then list all the positive benefits that will be received from the completion of your project. Remember, "All's well that begins well." Raise the level of your attitude!

ATTITUDE AXIOM #5:
OUR ATTITUDE CAN TURN OUR PROBLEMS INTO BLESSINGS.

In *Awake, My Heart*, my friend J. Sidlow Baxter writes, "What is the difference between an obstacle and an opportunity? Our attitude toward it. Every opportunity has a difficulty, and every difficulty has an opportunity."[1]

When confronted with a difficult situation, a person with an outstanding attitude makes the best of it while he gets the worst of it. Life can be likened to a grindstone. Whether it grinds you down or polishes you depends on what you are made of.

Few people knew Abraham Lincoln until the great weight of the Civil War showed his character. *Robinson Crusoe* was written in prison. John Bunyan wrote *Pilgrim's Progress* in the Bedford jail. Sir Walter Raleigh wrote *The History of the World* during a thirteen-year imprisonment. Luther translated the Bible while confined in the castle of Wartburg. Beethoven was almost totally deaf and burdened with sorrow when he produced his greatest works.

When God wants to educate a man, He does not send him to the school of graces but to the school of necessities. Through the pit and the dungeon, Joseph came to the throne. Moses tended sheep in the desert before God called him for service. Peter, humbled and broken by his denial of Christ, heeded the command to "Feed My sheep."

Great leaders emerge when crises occur. In the lives of people who achieve, terrible troubles force them to rise above the commonplace. Not only do they find the answers, but they discover a tremendous power within themselves. Like a groundswell far out in the ocean, this force within explodes into a mighty wave when circumstances seem to overcome. Then out steps the athlete, the author, the statesman, the scientist, or the businessman. David Sarnoff said, "There is plenty of security in the cemetery; I long for opportunity."

—————— Attitude Application ——————

List two problems that are presently a part of your life. Besides the two problems, write down your present reactions to them. Are they negative? Your challenge: Discover at least three possible benefits from each problem. Now attack the problems with your eyes on the benefits, not the barriers.

Attitude Axiom #6:
Our attitude can give us an uncommonly positive perspective.

The result of that truth: the accomplishment of uncommon goals. I have keenly observed the different approaches and results achieved by a positive thinker and by a person filled with fear and apprehension.

Example: When Goliath came up against the Israelites, the soldiers all thought, *He's so big we can never kill him.* David looked at the same giant and thought, *He's so big I can't miss.*

Moody Bible Institute president George Sweeting, in his sermon entitled "Attitude Makes the Difference," tells about a Scotsman who was an extremely hard worker and expected all the men under him to be the same. His men would tease him, "Scotty, don't you know that Rome wasn't built in a day?" "Yes," he would answer, "I know that. But I wasn't foreman on that job."

The people whose attitude causes them to approach life from an entirely positive perspective are not always understood. They are what some would call "no-limit" people. In other words, they don't accept the normal limitations of life like most people. They are unwilling to accept the accepted just because it is accepted. Their responses to self-limiting conditions will probably be a "Why?" instead of an "Okay." They have limitations in life. Their gifts are not so plentiful that they cannot fail. But they are determined to walk to the very edge of their potential or the potential of a project before they accept a defeat.

This mind-set allows a person to start each day with a positive disposition, like the elevator operator on Monday morning.

The elevator was full, and the man began humming a tune. One passenger seemed particularly irritated by the man's mood and snapped, "What are you so happy about?" "Well, sir," replied the man happily, "I ain't never lived this day before!"

The future not only looks bright when the attitude is right, but also the present is much more enjoyable. The positive person understands that the journey is as enjoyable as the destination.

——— Attitude Application ———

> Notice the limitation that you or your friends accept today.
> With each limitation example ask the question, Why?
> Example: "Why did I choose a parking space far away without checking up close first?" Make a mental note to become a "no-limit" person each time you ask the question, Why?

Attitude Axiom #7:
Our attitude is not automatically good just because we are Christians.

It is noteworthy that the seven deadly sins (pride, covetousness, lust, envy, anger, gluttony, and sloth) are all matters of attitude, inner spirit, and motives. Sadly, many carnal Christians carry with them inner spirit problems. They are like the elder brother of the prodigal son, thinking they do everything right. He chose to stay home with the father. No way was he going to spend his time sowing wild oats. Yet, when the younger brother came back home, some of the elder brother's wrong attitudes began to surface.

First came a feeling of self-importance. The elder brother was out in the field doing what he ought to do, but he got mad when the party began at home. He didn't get mad because he didn't like parties. I know he liked parties, because he complained to his father that he never got to throw one!

That was followed by a feeling of self-pity. The elder brother said, "Look! For so many years I have been serving you, and I have never neglected a command of yours; and yet you have never given me a kid, that I might be merry with my friends; but when this son of yours came, who has devoured your wealth with harlots, you killed the fatted calf for him" (Luke 15:29–30).

Often we overlook the true meaning of the story of the prodigal son. We forget that we have not one but two prodigals. The younger brother is guilty of the sins of the flesh, whereas the elder brother is guilty of the sins of the spirit (attitude). When the parable closes, it is the elder—the second prodigal—who is outside the father's house.

This "elder brother" attitude has three possible results, none of which is positive.

First, it is possible for us to assume the place and privilege of a son while refusing the obligations of a brother. The elder brother outwardly was correct, conscientious, industrious, and dutiful, but his attitude was wrong. Also note that a wrong relationship with the brother brought a strained relationship with the father (v. 28).

Second, it is possible to serve the Father faithfully yet not be in fellowship with Him. A right relationship will usually cultivate similar interests and priorities. Yet the elder brother had no idea why the father would rejoice over his son's return.

Third, it is possible to be an heir of all our Father possesses yet have less joy and liberty than one who possesses nothing. The servants were happier than the elder son. They ate, laughed, and danced while he stood on the outside demanding his rights.

A wrong attitude kept the elder brother away from the heart's desire of the father, the love of his brother, and the joy of the servants. Wrong attitudes in our lives will block the blessings of God and cause us to live below God's potential for our lives.

———— ## Attitude Application ————

When our attitude begins to erode like the elder brother's, we should remember two things:

1. Our privilege: "My child, you have always been with me" (v. 31).
2. Our possessions: "All that is mine is yours" (v. 31).

Take a moment to list your privileges and possessions in Christ. How rich we are!

THE CONSTRUCTION
OF YOUR ATTITUDE

4

It's Hard to Soar with the
Eagles When You Have to
Live with the Turkeys

O ur surroundings control our soaring. Turkey-thinking
+ turkey-talk = turkey-walk. We quickly blend into the
color of our surroundings. Similarities in thinking, mannerisms, priorities, talk, and opinions are very common within
individual cultures. We all know married people who grow to
look more alike as the years pass. Many times family members
exhibit similar physical traits.

Unquestionably our surroundings help construct our attitudes too.

The word *choices* rises on the opposite side of environment in the attitude construction issue. Speaking more logically than emotionally, the voice of this word says, "We are free to choose our attitudes." This logic becomes more convincing with the additional voice of Victor Frankl, survivor of a Nazi concentration camp, who said, "The last of the human freedoms is to choose one's attitude in *any* given set of circumstances."

In our early years, our attitudes are determined mainly by our conditions. A baby does not choose her family or her environment, but as her age increases, so do her options.

Awhile ago I conducted a leadership seminar in Columbus, Ohio. For an entire day I talked about the importance of attitudes and about how many times they make the difference in our lives. During one of the breaks, a man told me the following story:

> From my earliest recollections I do not remember a compliment or affirmation from my father. His father also had thought it unmanly to express affection or even appreciation. My grandfather was a perfectionist who worked hard and expected everyone else to do the same without positive reinforcement. And since he was neither positive nor relational, he had constant turnover in employees.
>
> Because of my background, it has been difficult for me to encourage my family. This critical and negative attitude has hindered my work. I raised five children and lived a Christian life before them. Sadly, it is easier for them to recognize my love for God than my love for them. They are all starved for positive affirmation. The tragedy is that they have received the bad attitude trait, and now I see them passing it down to my precious grandchildren.
>
> Never before have I been so aware of "catching an attitude" from surrounding conditions. Obviously, this wrong attitude has been passed along for five generations. It is now

time to stop it! Today I made a conscious decision to change. This will not be done overnight, but it will be done. It will not be accomplished easily, but it will be accomplished!

That story contains both the conditions that mold our thinking and the choice to change. Both play a vital part in the construction of our attitude. Neither can be held solely responsible for forming our mind-set.

—— Attitude Application ——

List the conditions that have had positive and negative influences on your life (i.e., in a particular situation, you chose to find the good in the circumstance or you viewed the matter with humor).

Conditions		Choices	
Positive:	*Negative:*	*Positive:*	*Negative:*

5

Foundational Truths About the
Construction of the Attitude

B efore we look at specific things that help construct attitudes, we must understand some basic principles about
attitude formation.

1. A CHILD'S FORMATIVE YEARS ARE THE MOST IMPORTANT FOR INSTILLING THE RIGHT ATTITUDES.

Child specialists generally agree that early development in a
positive setting is a main reason for the child's future successes.
Attitudes we accept as children are usually the attitudes we
embrace as adults. It is hard to get away from our early training.

Proverbs 22:6 states, "Train up a child in the way he should go, even when he is old he will not depart from it." Why? Because the feeling and attitudes we form early in life become a part of us. We feel comfortable with them even though they may be wrong. Even if our attitudes make us uncomfortable, they are still difficult to change.

2. An attitude's growth never stops.

Our attitudes are formed by our experiences and how we choose to react to them. Therefore, as long as we live, we are forming, changing, or reinforcing attitudes. There is no such thing as an unalterable attitude. We are like the little girl who was asked by her Sunday school teacher, "Who made you?" She replied, "Well, God made part of me." "What do you mean, God made part of you?" asked the surprised teacher. "Well, God made me real little, and I just growed the rest myself."

How true! The attitudes formed in our early years do not necessarily remain the same through later years. Many times marriages go through "deep waters" because of a mate's attitude change. People sometimes even switch spouses in the middle of life because of an attitude change.

3. The more our attitude grows on the same foundation, the more solid it becomes.

Reinforcement of our foundational attitudes, whether positive or negative, makes them stronger. My father realized this truth in his commitment to read his positive-thinking books again. One of his attitude-growing practices was to write a positive thought on a 3 x 5 card and read it repeatedly throughout the day. Often I have seen him pull out the card during fifteen-second breaks and read the positive phrase. I have decided to make this a habit of mine also. I find that the more I reinforce my mind with excellent reading, the stronger I become.

4. MANY BUILDERS (SPECIALISTS) HELP CONSTRUCT OUR ATTITUDES AT A CERTAIN TIME AND PLACE.

In building a home, certain specialists are needed to make the structure complete. Their time may be minimal and their contribution small, yet they are a part of the construction of that home. In the same way, certain people come into our lives at various times who help make or break our perspective.

5. THERE IS NO SUCH THING AS A PERFECT, FLAWLESS ATTITUDE.

In other words, we all have attitudes that need remodeling. When he taught me about airplanes, my friend Paul stated, "An aircraft hasn't been made that did not have to be trimmed." The word *trim* means to "balance in flight." Airplanes need continual adjustment in order to perform effectively. This is true of our attitudes also. The air currents of life jolt us out of line and try to keep us from achieving our goals. Unexpected weather can change our direction and strategy. Our attitudes need adjustment with every change that comes into our lives.

Everyone encounters storms in his life that threaten to wreck his attitude. The secret to safe arrival is to continually adjust your perspective.

—————— Attitude Application ——————

Our attitude does not remain stagnant. A balloon half blown up is full of air but is not filled to capacity. A rubber band pulls the object it holds together and is effective only when stretched. What are you encountering that demands the stretching of your attitude? Are you adjusting? Write a statement that identifies what you feel will be your next "storm." Now think through the strategy you'll use to counter a possible bad attitude regarding that situation.

6

Materials That Are Used in Constructing an Attitude

As you're probably aware by this time, attitudes aren't formed automatically, and they are not shaped in a vacuum. This chapter will deal with the main influences that make our attitudes what they are today. Although these "materials," listed below in chronological order, overlap, their influence is greater at some times than at others.

Personality/Temperament

BIRTH:	*Environment*
AGES 1–6:	*Word expression*
	Adult acceptance / affirmation
AGES 7–10:	*Self-image*
	Exposure to new experiences
AGES 11–21:	*Associations with peers*
	Physical appearance
AGES 22–61:	*Marriage, family, job*
	Success
	Adjustments
	Assessment of life

All these factors play an important part in our lives and cannot really be "boxed" into age zones. As indicated above, there are certain ages when these factors are most influential.

——— Attitude Application ———

Take time to think through the materials that have constructed your attitudes. Write down your answers.

Personality/Temperament: I was born into this world with a _____ personality. It affected my attitude when _____.

Environment: As a child my environment was generally (a) secure, (b) unstable, (c) intimidating.

Word Expression: Remember a situation when someone said something positive or negative to me that affected my attitude. Explain the comment and the circumstances.

_____

_____

Adult Acceptance / Affirmation: From my earliest recollection I felt (a) accepted or (b) rejected by my parents.

Self-Image: Poor   Outstanding
My self-image as a child was: 1   2   3   4   5
My self-image as an adult is: 1   2   3   4   5

Exposure to New Experiences: One negative and one positive experience that helped cultivate my current attitude:

_____

_____

Association with Peers: _____ was the first person who had a strong influence in my life. Now _____ is most important and affects my attitude the most.

Physical Appearance: What do I like best about my appearance? What would I change? Why?

_____

_____

Marriage, Family, Job: (These three areas of your life can determine your attitude to a large degree.) Which area affects me positively? Do any affect me negatively? What am I going to do about the negative influences?

Success: Success is

_____

Am I a success in the eyes of those who love me most?

_____

Adjustments—Physical and Emotional: Three difficult adjustments that I have faced within the last five years are

_____
_____
_____

How has my attitude changed because of them?

_____

Assessment of Your Life: Until now, my life has been (a) unfulfilled or (b) fulfilled. Life begins at

_____.

Now that you've assessed how your perspective was affected in various phases of life, let's look at the specific materials that form your attitude.

Personality—Who I Am

We are born as distinct individuals. Even two children with the same parents, same environments, and same training are totally different from one another. These differences contribute to the "spice of life" we all enjoy. Like tract homes that all look alike, if all people had similar personalities, our journey through life certainly would be boring.

A set of attitudes accompanies each personality. Generally people with certain temperaments develop specific attitudes common to that temperament. Years ago, pastor and counselor Tim LaHaye made us aware of four basic temperaments.[1] Through observation, I have noticed that a person with what he calls a Choleric personality often exhibits attitudes of perseverance and aggressiveness. A Sanguine person is generally positive and looks on the bright side of life. The introspective Melancholy can be negative at times, while the Phlegmatic says, "Easy come, easy go." An individual's personality is composed of a mixture of these temperaments, and there are exceptions to these examples. However, a temperament follows a track that can be identified by tracing a person's attitudes.

ENVIRONMENT—WHAT'S AROUND ME

I believe that our environment is a greater controlling factor in our attitude development than our personality or other inherited traits. Before Margaret and I began our family, we decided to adopt our children. We wanted to give a child who might not normally have the benefit of a loving home an opportunity to live in that environment. Although our children may not physically resemble us, they certainly were molded by the environment in which we reared them.

Environment is the first influencer of our belief system. Therefore, the foundation of our attitude is laid in the environment in which we were born. Environment becomes even more significant when we realize that *the beginning attitudes are the most difficult to change*. Because of this, when we look at society, we have a tendency to panic over the thought of bringing a child into this world.

A Christian should not view society so negatively. With Jesus, life becomes incredible! Knowing this gives hope in every environment. The apostle Peter said that the mercy of Christ has caused us to be born to "a living hope" (1 Peter 1:3).

Still, age and Christianity do not make us immune to the influences of our environment. I pastored Faith Memorial Church in Lancaster, Ohio, for more than seven years. I remember 1978 as the year central Ohio received many baptisms of snow and cold weather. For more than thirty days the temperature never rose above freezing. People became claustrophobic as they were snowed in for days. The result: depression. I averaged thirty hours a week counseling people who battled attitude problems because of bad weather. Even the weather can "ice our wings" and cause us to lose altitude in our attitude.

Word Expression—What I Hear

"Sticks and stones may break my bones, but words will never hurt me."

Don't you believe that! In fact, after the bruises have disappeared and the physical pain is gone, the inward pain of hurtful words remains. During a staff meeting at Skyline, I asked the pastors, assistants, and custodians to raise their hands if they could remember a childhood experience that hurt deeply because of someone's words. Everyone raised his hand.

One pastor recalled the time when he sat in a reading circle at school. When his time came to read, he mispronounced the word *photography*. The teacher corrected him, and the class laughed. He still remembers . . . forty years later. One positive result of that experience was Chuck's desire from that moment on to pronounce words correctly. Today he excels as a speaker because of that determination.

Words are powerful, yet meaningless until they are attached to a concept. The same words coming from two different people are very seldom received the same way. The same words phrased differently seldom have the same impact. The same words coming from the same person will usually be interpreted in light of the speaker's attitude. One mother tried to teach her son this truth. One day the boy came home and said, "Mom, I think I flunked my math test." His mom said, "Son, don't say that; that's negative. Be positive." So the boy said, "Mom, I am positive I flunked my math test."

ADULT ACCEPTANCE /
AFFIRMATION—WHAT I FEEL

Often when I am speaking to leaders, I tell them about the importance of acceptance and affirmation of the ones they are leading. The truth is *people don't care how much you know until they know how much you care*!

Think back to your school days. Who was your favorite teacher? Why? Probably your warmest memories are of someone who accepted and affirmed you. We seldom remember what our teachers said to us, but we do remember how they loved us. Long before we understand teaching, we reach out for understanding. Long after we have forgotten the teachings, we remember the feeling of acceptance or rejection.

Many times I have asked people if they enjoyed their pastors' sermons the previous week. After a positive response, I ask, "What was his subject?" Seventy-five percent of the time, they cannot give me the sermon title. They do not remember the exact subject, but they do remember the atmosphere and the attitude in which it was delivered.

I once talked with Mary Vaughn, who was once the head of counseling in the Cincinnati elementary school system. I asked her to pinpoint the main problem she noticed in counseling situations. "John," she said immediately, "most children's psychological problems stem from their lack of acceptance and affirmation from parents and peers." Mary continually emphasized that economic level, professional or social strata, and other factors in which society puts so much value were insignificant.

Then she told me about Dennis, aged ten. This third grader was always fighting, lying, and causing disturbances with his classmates. He believed "no one likes me, the teacher just picks on me." He would not respond to the people who really cared for him and tried to help the most. His problem? He wanted his mother's affirmation and love so much that he lived in a fantasy world, always talking of his mother's love. In reality, his mother did nothing to affirm him. Dennis's need for care was so great that he fantasized about his mother's love and directed his bad attitude toward others.

Unlike Dennis, I was privileged to grow up in a very affirming family. I never questioned my parents' love and acceptance. They were continually affirming their love through actions and words. Margaret and I tried to create this same environment for our children. We often talked about the importance of showing love to our children. We concluded that kids see or sense our acceptance and affirmation at least thirty times a day. That's not too much! Have you ever been told too many times that you are important, loved, and appreciated? Remember *people don't care how much you know until they know how much you care.*

Self-Image—How I See Myself

It is impossible to perform consistently in a manner inconsistent with the way we see ourselves. In other words, we usually act in direct response to our self-image. Nothing is more difficult to accomplish than changing outward actions without changing inward feelings. As we realize our performance is based on our perception of ourselves, we should also remember God's unconditional love and acceptance. He thinks more of us than we do of ourselves. The disciples may not have been high achievers in the sight of the world, but the call of Christ turned their lives around.

One of the best ways to improve those inward feelings is to put some "success" under your belt. My daughter Elizabeth had a tendency to be shy and wanted to hold back on new experiences. But once she warmed up to a situation, it was "full steam ahead." When she was in the first grade, her school had a candy bar sale to help lift its financial burden. Each child was given thirty candy bars and was challenged to sell every one of them. When I picked Elizabeth up from school, she was holding her "challenge" and needed some positive encouragement. It was time for a sales meeting with my new salesgirl.

All the way home I taught her how to sell candy bars. I surrounded each teaching point with a half dozen "You can do it—Your smile will win them over—I believe in you" phrases. By the end of our fifteen-minute drive, the young lady sitting beside me had become a charming, committed salesperson. Off she went to the neighborhood with little brother Joel eating one of the candy bars.

At the end of the day, all thirty bars had been sold, and Elizabeth was feeling great. I will never forget the words she prayed as I tucked her into bed that night: "O God, thanks for the candy bar sale at school. It's great. O Lord, help make me a winner! Amen."

This prayer is the heart's desire of every person. We want to be winners. Sure enough, Elizabeth came home the next day with another box of candy bars. Now the best test! She'd exhausted the supply of friendly neighbors, and she was thrust out into the cruel world of the unknown buyer. Elizabeth admitted fear as we went to a shopping center to sell our wares. Again I offered encouragement, a few more selling tips, more encouragement, the right location, *more* encouragement. She did it. The experience amounted to two days of selling, two sold-out performances, two happy people, and one boosted self-image.

This principle works in reverse too. How we see ourselves reflects how others see us. If we like ourselves, it increases the odds that others will like us. *Self-image is the parameter to the construction of our attitude.* We act in response to how we see ourselves. We will never go beyond the boundaries that stake out our true feelings about ourselves. Those "other countries" can be explored only when our self-image is strong enough to give permission.

Exposure to New Experiences— Opportunities for Growth

Voltaire likened life to a game of cards. Each player must accept the cards dealt to him. But once those cards are in the hand, he alone decides how to play them to win the game.

We always have a number of opportunities in our hands. We must decide whether to take a risk and act on them. Nothing in life causes more stress, yet at the same time provides more opportunity for growth, than new experiences.

My parents recognized the value of new experiences and did their best to expose each child to positive ones. Some of my fondest memories are of times when I traveled with my father. Many times he would say to my teacher, "You are doing an excellent job teaching my son, but for the next week I am going to take him with me and open up some new experiences for him." Off we would go to another state, and my awareness of people, nature, and culture would be heightened.

I will always be especially grateful for those prearranged new experiences. I'll never forget the time I met the great missionary statesman E. Stanley Jones. After listening to this spiritual giant speak, my father took me to a side office to meet him! I can still remember the room, his attitude, and, most important, his words of encouragement to me.

As a parent, it is impossible for you to shield your children from the new experiences that might be negative. So it is essential to prepare positive encounters that will build self-image and confidence. Both positive and negative experiences should be used as tools in preparing children for life.

Elizabeth's story didn't end after two successful selling days. Later she went door-to-door again, encouraging people to buy the "world's most delicious chocolate bar." I followed her in the car. We set a goal (the end of a very long block) and determined not to quit until that goal was reached.

With each "no sale" visit her steps became slower and my enthusiasm greater. Finally she made a sale at the next to the last house. She came running back to the car, waving money and wanting to go one more block. I said, "Fine," and off she ran.

The lesson is obvious. Children need continual reassurance and praise when their new experiences are less than positive. In fact, the worse the experience, the more encouragement they need. But sometimes we become discouraged when they are discouraged. The following is a good formula to adopt:

New experiences + teaching applications × love = growth.

ASSOCIATION WITH PEERS—WHO INFLUENCES ME

What others indicate about their perceptions of us affects how we perceive ourselves. Usually we respond to the expectations of others. This truth becomes evident to the parent when his child goes to school. No longer can the parent control his child's environment. Any elementary teacher understands that kids very quickly develop a "pecking order" for the class. Students acquire labels, and children relate to each other with sometimes cruel honesty. Peer pressure becomes a problem.

Mary Vaughn, in one of her case studies involving a first grader, wrote, "A very poor environment physically (little clothing, shelter, or food) does not necessarily produce negative attitudes in the child. It is the lack of acceptance by peers that forms scars deep within the child." Her example—a first grader who was stealing.

Terry looked pale and sickly. The teacher was concerned about his stealing. Missing things were usually found in his desk. After counseling with Terry, a home visit was arranged with his parents. Their dwelling contained four rooms and housed nine people. The rooms were scarcely furnished, and poverty was evident. The parents were grateful for the offer of assistance and clothing. They were also willing to help Terry. Assessment of the problem: Terry stole only because peer pressure made him aware of his poverty. He wanted the same cute erasers and lunch boxes his friends had. No doubt this experience helped Terry's parents realize that others exercised a sizable amount of control over their son's behavior.

Casey Stengel, a successful manager of the New York Yankees baseball team, understood the power of associations on a ball player's attitude. Billy Martin remembered Stengel's advice to him when Martin was a rookie manager. "Casey said there would be fifteen players on your team who will run through a wall for you, five who will hate you, and five who are undecided," Martin said. Stengel added, "When you make out your rooming list, always room your losers together. Never room a good guy with a loser. Those losers who stay together will blame the manager for everything, but it won't spread if you keep them isolated."

At one meeting a man came up to me after I had spoken about attitudes and associates. He wanted me to clarify the concept of isolating ourselves from others who can drag us down. His question was, "How can we help others who have attitude problems if we stay away from them?" My answer: "There is a difference between helping those with perpetual attitude problems and enlisting them as our close friends. The closer our relationship, the more influential the attitudes and philosophies of our friends become to us."

PHYSICAL APPEARANCE—HOW WE LOOK TO OTHERS

Our appearance plays an important part in the construction of our attitude. Incredible pressure is placed upon people to possess that "in" look that is the standard of acceptance. For one day, while you're watching television notice how the commercials emphasize looks. Notice the percentage of ads dealing with clothing, diet, exercise, and overall physical attractiveness. Hollywood says, "Homeliness is out and handsomeness is in." This influences our perception of our worth, based on physical appearance. What can make it even more difficult is the realization that others judge our worth also by our appearance. Years ago I read a business article that stated, "Our physical attractiveness helps determine our income." The research reported in that article showed the discrepancies between the salaries of men 6'2" and 5'10". The taller men consistently received higher salaries.

MARRIAGE, FAMILY, AND JOB— OUR SECURITY AND STATUS

New influences begin to affect our attitude as we approach our midtwenties. It is during this time of our lives that most of us marry. That means another person influences our perspective.

When I speak on attitudes, I always emphasize the need to surround ourselves with positive people. One of the saddest comments that I often receive comes from one mate who tells me the other marriage partner is negative and doesn't want to change. To a certain extent, when the negative mate does not want to change, the positive one is imprisoned by negativism. In such situations, I advise the couple to remember and return to patterns they followed in their courtship days.

Observe a couple during courtship. They are illustrating two beautiful ideas. They are building on strengths and expecting the best. This is when a girl tends to see the guy as a knight in shining armor. She's looking for his best. She's expecting his best. She ignores anything that seems to be a weakness. The man sees a beautiful girl with noble feelings and fine qualities. Then they get married, and each one sees the reality of the other—both strengths and weaknesses. The marriage will be good and reinforcing if the weaknesses are not emphasized. But many end up in divorce court because the strengths are ignored. The partners go from expecting the best to expecting the worst, from building on strengths to focusing on weaknesses.

Whether you are eleven, forty-two, or sixty-five, your attitude toward life is still under construction. By understanding the materials that are part of your attitude structures, you and those you influence can maintain a healthier perspective.

7

The Costliest Mistake People
Make in Constructing an Attitude

It happens to us the moment we are born. Excited family members press their noses against the nursery window in the hospital and begin playing the game, "Who does he look like?" After much discussion, it is decided that their red-faced, wrinkly, toothless baby looks like "Uncle Harry."

The labeling of the little child increases as her personality develops. That is a normal human reaction. We all do it. It becomes hurtful, however, when we start placing limitations on our child because he is a "C" student, a "fair" runner, or a "plain" child. Unless parents exercise care, their children will grow up selling themselves short because of the "box" parents have put them in, the expectations parents have placed upon them.

What are a person's capabilities? No one knows. Therefore, no one should be consciously instilling life-limiting thoughts onto others. Many years ago, Johnny Weissmuller, also known as Tarzan to movie viewers, was called the greatest swimmer the world had ever known. Doctors and coaches around the world said, "Nobody will ever break Johnny Weissmuller's records." He held more than fifty of them! Do you know who is breaking Tarzan's records today? Thirteen-year-old girls! The 1936 Olympic records were the *qualifying* standards for the 1972 Olympics.

Remember: Others can stop you temporarily, but you are the only one who can do it permanently.

An elephant can easily pick up a one-ton load with his trunk. But have you ever visited a circus and watched these huge creatures standing quietly tied to a small wooden stake?

While still young and weak, an elephant is tied by a heavy chain to an immovable iron stake. He discovers that no matter how hard he tries, he cannot break the chain or move the stake. Then, no matter how large and strong the elephant becomes, he continues to believe he cannot move as long as he sees the stake in the ground beside him.

Many intelligent adults behave like the circus elephant. They are restrained in thought, action, and results. They never move further than the boundaries of self-imposed limitation.

Often when lecturing on limitations, I talk about what I call the "sap strata."

Our Potential

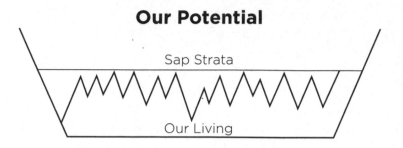

Sap Strata

Our Living

In this illustration, the sap strata line represents our self-imposed, limiting barrier. The jagged line that keeps rising and falling pictures our actual living. The effort it would take to break through that sap strata level takes the "sap" out of us. Every time we make an attempt to break through the line, there is accompanying pain. We pay a physical and emotional price when we actually break through our perceived limitations and enter into a new area of further potential.

Later, in sections III and IV of this book, we will take a closer look at the process. Sadly, many people accept their sap strata and never reach their potential. They are like the trained fleas that jump up and down in a canister. The observant bystander will notice that the jar has no lid to keep the fleas inside. So why don't those fleas jump out of the container to their freedom? The answer is simple. The flea trainer, when first placing the fleas into the canister, also puts the lid on top. The fleas jump high and continually bash their little flea brains on the lid. After a few "Excedrin headaches," the fleas quit jumping so high and enjoy their newfound comfort. Now the lid can be removed, and the fleas are held captive; not by a real lid, but by a mind-set that says, "So high and no more."

I've listed below a few comments we unthinkingly make that can limit potential and keep us from breaking through the sap strata:

"It's never been done before."
"I'll never try that again."
"Take it easy."

Now it's your turn. Make a list of statements that have limited your potential.

If someone tries to saddle you with sap strata, here's a poem that can counter the attack. Read it from time to time.

> Somebody said that it couldn't be done,
> But he with a chuckle replied
> That maybe it couldn't, but he would be one
> Who wouldn't say no till he tried. . . .
> Just start to sing as you tackle the thing
> That "cannot be done," and you'll do it.[1]
>
> —*Edgar A. Guest*

THE CRASHING OF YOUR ATTITUDE

8

⟡⟡⟡

Mayday! Mayday! My Attitude Is Losing Altitude

One of the first things I discovered during my ride in a small airplane was that turbulence often makes the ride a little rough. Just as flying has its rough weather, so does life. A smooth day is the exception, not the norm. Flying straight and level usually comes as a *recovery* from climbs, descents, and turns. It's the exception, not the rule.

Have you ever had a day like the small boy had in *Alexander and the Terrible, Horrible, No Good, Very Bad Day*, by Judith Viorst?

I went to bed with gum in my mouth and now there's gum in my hair and when I got out of bed this morning I tripped on the skateboard and by mistake I dropped my sweater in the sink while the water was running and I could tell it was going to be a terrible, horrible, no good, very bad day.[1]

Here are some rules to remember when you have one of those terrible, horrible, no good, very bad days and your attitude starts to plummet.

Rule 1:
Maintain the right attitude when the "going gets tough."

Our natural reaction is to bail out of the right attitude to compensate for our problems. During our flight of life, our attitude is most critical during the "tough times." That is when we are tempted to panic and make bad attitude decisions. When we crash, it comes from a wrong reaction, not the turbulence. How often have we seen the "making a mountain out of a molehill" response become more dangerous than the problem itself?

Remember, the difficulty really becomes a problem when we internalize unfortunate circumstances. Another thing to remember when the weather gets rough is that *what really matters is what happens in us, not to us!* When the external circumstances lead to wrong internal reactions, we really have problems.

I once talked to a man who was having financial difficulty. He faced the prospect of losing everything. I offered prayer and encouragement during this difficult time. His reaction: "I've never been closer to God!" He told how this trial was making him stronger in his walk with God. Paul told Timothy that Christians would be persecuted. He said that not only had he endured persecution but also that God had always delivered him

(2 Tim. 3:11–12). Paul allowed the storms of life to strengthen him. How different from those who yell, "I quit!" every time difficulty arises.

RULE 2:
REALIZE THAT THE "ROUGH WEATHER" WILL NOT LAST FOREVER.

When you're caught in the middle of touchy situations, it is often difficult to remember this truth. We become consumed with the problems. Our entire outlook is colored by the present. A drowning person is not concerned about tomorrow's schedule.

There is an expression I use quite often when I sense that the difficulties of the day are overwhelming me. At the moment when I have "had enough," I say, "This too shall pass!" That brief statement really works. It helps me gain perspective on my situation.

Many times I have heard runners talk about the "highs" they receive in running. (It is hard to convince me of their claim when I observe the grimaces on their faces as they run.) Once they receive their "second wind," they feel like they could run all day. Their secret? Run until you get your second wind. The first part is difficult and painful. The last part is easier and fruitful.

RULE 3:
TRY TO MAKE MAJOR DECISIONS BEFORE THE STORM.

Many storms can be avoided by thinking and planning ahead. A pilot will check the weather in his planned flight before he makes his decision to proceed. When flying, he will check his radar or call ahead to anticipate weather conditions.

Obviously, not all storms can be avoided. Yet I wonder how

many we encounter because we fail to check all the resources available to us. Too many times our troubles are a result of our own poor planning and not the conditions that surround our lives.

To avoid some potential storms in life, we need to know and rely on rough weather indicators. I've listed some possible "eyes" that can help us foresee trouble and questions we should ask before proceeding toward solving the problem:

ROUGH WEATHER INDICATORS:	QUESTIONS TO ASK MYSELF:
Lack of experience	*Do I know someone with successful experience in this area?*
Lack of knowledge	*Have I studied sufficiently to direct my course effectively?*
Lack of time	*Did I allow the process of time to work on me as well as the storm?*
Lack of facts	*Are all the facts gathered to allow a proper decision?*
Lack of prayer	*Is this idea God's or mine? If mine, does God bless it and back it through His Word?*

Even after all weather indicators have been checked, we will still probably encounter some storms. Life's difficulties have a crazy way of sneaking up on us. When that happens, try to delay as many major decisions as possible. Our life is a series of "ups and downs." (See illustration on the following page.) There is one major difference between people who jump from one major problem to another and those who go from one major success to the next. The difference is timing.

Those who make one bad decision after another make their major decisions during the "lows" of life. Those who exhibit the

"Midas touch" have learned to wait until the "lows" pass and they feel on top of things.

When do you make the big "D"?

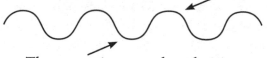

The right time to make a decision

The wrong time to make a decision

I cringe when I hear seminar speakers say, "It is more important to make the wrong decision immediately than to make no decision." Don't you believe it! The key to success in decision making is as much timing as making the right choice.

The wrong decision at the wrong time = disaster
The wrong decision at the right time = mistake
The right decision at the wrong time = unacceptance
The right decision at the right time = success

Usually wrong decisions are made at the wrong time, and right decisions are made at the right time. The reason? We let our environment control our thinking, which controls our decisions. Therefore, the more decisions that are made in the calm of life, the fewer times storms can bring us down.

RULE 4:
KEEP IN CONTACT WITH THE CONTROL TOWER.

Every pilot knows the value of communicating with knowledgeable people during times of trouble. The natural reaction when having difficulty in the sky is to radio for help. We do not always do this in our daily living.

Our tendency is often to try to make it on our own. We admire that rugged, independent individual who "pulled himself up by his bootstraps." That is the American way. At times we are all little Frank Sinatras belting out for all to hear, "I did it my way."

Jesus sings a different song. Its words speak about fullness of joy and fruitfulness. The thesis of His song states, "Apart from Me you can do nothing" (John 15:5). The title of His song is "Abide in Me and I in You" or, more modernly stated, "You'll Be Fine If You're Connected to the Vine."

Stanza 1 says, "Abide in Me, and I in you. As the branch cannot bear fruit of itself, unless it abides in the vine, so neither can you unless you abide in Me" (John 15:4).

Stanza 2 says, "I am the Vine, you are the branches; he who abides in Me, and I in him, he bears much fruit; for apart from Me you can do nothing" (John 15:5).

Stanza 3 says, "If anyone does not abide in Me, he is thrown away as a branch, and dries up; and they gather them and cast them into the fire, and they are burned" (John 15:6).

Stanza 4 says, "If you abide in Me, and My words abide in you, ask whatever you wish, and it shall be done for you" (John 15:7).

During a time of revival at Skyline, God began dealing with me about Jesus' statement, "Apart from Me, you can do nothing." I have always been prone to think, *Apart from God I can only do some things.* I would quickly admit my need for Him to do exceed "abundantly beyond all that we ask or think" (Eph. 3:20), but that which was less than extraordinary I felt sufficient to accomplish by myself. I learned that I can fly solo in my world no longer. Whether I'm in rough weather or in calm blue skies, I must keep in contact with Christ.

Attitude Application

Please read the following statements. Take a moment to apply these truths to your present attitude.

1. "What really matters is what happens in us, not to us."
   Which is more important: wrong action directed at me or wrong reaction within me?
   Why?

2. "What we sow, we always reap."
   Is that true?
   If not, why?

3. "The difference between success and failure in decision making is often timing."
   When does a winner make his or her decisions?
   When do I make mine?

We talked about factors that cause us to lose altitude. The following chapters of section III are "crash causers." These are either the things that cause us to crash or the things we blame when we make uncomfortable landings.

9

The Crash from Within

There are certain storms within a person's life that contribute to an attitude crash. The three storms I'm discussing in this chapter are predominantly inward, not outward. They are part of us and must be constructively dealt with to bring inner peace and a wholesome attitude.

The Fear of Failure

The first inward storm is: the *fear of failure*.

We have had many ways of dealing with it. Some people determine, "If at first you don't succeed, destroy all the evidence that you've tried."

Failure—We hide it,
        deny it,
        fear it,
        ignore it, and
        hate it.

We do everything but accept it. By acceptance, I don't mean resignation and apathy. I mean understanding that failure is a necessary step to success. The person who never makes a mistake never does anything.

I enjoy reading about the lives of great individuals. One consistent fact I notice is all successful people experienced failure. In fact, most of them began as failures.

When the great Polish pianist Ignace Paderewski first chose to study the piano, his music teacher told him his hands were much too small to master the keyboard.

When the great Italian tenor Enrico Caruso first applied for instruction, the teacher told him his voice sounded like the wind whistling through the window.

Henry Ford forgot to put a reverse gear in his first car.

Thomas Edison spent two million dollars on an invention that proved to be of little value.

Very little comes out right the first time. Failures, repeated failures, are fingerprints on the road to achievement.

Accepting failure in the positive sense becomes effective when you believe that the right to fail is as important as the right to succeed. When I lived in San Diego, I enjoyed the weather more than the Southern California natives. Why? Because I had lived in Ohio and experienced the winter of '78, not to mention a few others. Exposure to problems gives greater joy in our progress if we can accept failure as an important process in reaching our goals.

It is impossible to succeed without suffering. If you are successful and have not suffered, someone has suffered for you, and if you are suffering without succeeding, perhaps someone may succeed after you. But there is not success without suffering.

Take a risk. Climb out on a limb where the fruit is. Too many people are still hugging the tree trunk, wondering why they are not receiving the fruit of life. Many potential leaders never achieved because they stood back and let someone else take the risk. Many potential recipients never received because they didn't step out of the crowd and ask. James tells us "we have not because we ask not" (James 4:2). Realistically, we ask not because we fear rejection. Therefore, we take no risk.

But risk must be taken, because the greatest hazard in life is to risk nothing. The person who risks nothing does nothing, has nothing, and is nothing. He may avoid suffering and sorrow, but he simply cannot learn, grow, feel, change, love, or live. Chained by his certitudes, he is a slave: he has forfeited freedom.

Fear of failure grips those who take themselves too seriously. While we were growing up, many of us spent a great deal of time worrying about what the world thinks of us. By the time we reach middle age, we realize that the world wasn't paying much attention all that time we were worrying. Until we accept the fact that the future of the world does not hinge on our decisions, we will be unable to forget past mistakes.

Attitude is the determining factor of whether our failures make us or break us. The persistence of a person who encounters failure is one sign of a healthy attitude. Winners don't quit! Failure becomes devastating and causes our attitude to crash when we quit. To accept failure as final is to be finally a failure.

————— Attitude Application —————

Read these reinforcing thoughts about dealing with failure. Write them on 3 x 5 cards and keep them visible so you can read them often.

The man who never makes a mistake never makes anything.

Failures, repeated failures, are fingerprints on the road to achievement.

It is impossible to succeed without suffering.

Attitude is the determining factor of whether our failures make or break us.

To accept failure as final is to be finally a failure.

The Dread of Discouragement

The second storm within us that causes attitude crash is: the *dread of discouragement.*

Elijah is one of my favorite Bible characters. Never has a man of God enjoyed a greater moment than his experience at Mt. Carmel. Boldness, faith, power, obedience, and effective prayer describe Elijah as he stood with the worshipers of Baal. But deliverance (1 Kings 18) was followed by discouragement (1 Kings 19). His attitude went from boldness before God to blaming God for his trouble. Fear replaced faith. Power was drained by pity, and disobedience replaced obedience. How quickly things changed! Sound familiar? Turn to 1 Kings 19 and notice the four thoughts on discouragement.

First, discouragement hurts our self-image:

But he himself went on a day's journey into the wilderness, and came and sat down under a juniper tree; and he requested for himself that he might die, and said "It is enough; now, O Lord, take my life, for I am not better than my fathers" (v. 4).

Discouragement causes us to see ourselves as less than we really are. This fact becomes even more important when we realize that we cannot consistently perform in a manner that is inconsistent with the way we see ourselves.

Second, discouragement causes us to evade our responsibilities:

> Then he came there to a cave, and lodged there; and behold the word of the LORD came to him, and He said to him, "What are you doing here, Elijah?" (v. 9).

The Elijahs of life are created for Mt. Carmels, not caves. Faith brings us to ministry. Fear hands us only misery.

Third, discouragement causes us to blame others for our predicaments:

> And he said, "I have been very zealous for the LORD, the God of hosts; for the sons of Israel have forsaken Your covenant, torn down Your altars and killed Your prophets with the sword. And I alone am left; and they seek my life, to take it away." (v. 10).

Fourth, discouragement causes us to blur the facts:

> Yet I will leave 7,000 in Israel, all the knees that have not bowed to Baal and every mouth that has not kissed him (v. 18).

From only one to seven thousand. No doubt about it: discouragement had done a number on this great prophet. And if it can happen to great men, what about us? What about others? Discouragement is contagious.

We are all subject to the currents of discouragement that can sweep us into a danger zone. If we know some of the causes of discouragement, we can more easily avoid it. Discouragement comes when we:

1. Feel that opportunity for success is gone.

The test of your character is seeing what it takes to stop you. We need the spirit of the boy in the Little League. A man stopped to watch a Little League baseball game. He asked one of the youngsters the score.

"We're behind eighteen to nothing," was the answer.

"Well," said the man, "I must say you don't look discouraged."

"Discouraged?" the boy asked. "Why should we be discouraged? We haven't come to bat yet."

2. Become selfish.

Usually people who are discouraged are thinking about one thing—themselves.

3. Are not immediately successful in our attempts to do something.

A study conducted by the National Retail Dry Goods Association pointed out that unsuccessful first attempts lead almost half of all salesmen to certain failure. Note:

48 percent of all salesmen make one call and stop.
25 percent of all salesmen make two calls and stop.
15 percent of all salesmen make three calls and stop.
12 percent of all salesmen go back and back and back and back.
They make 80 percent of all sales.

We conquer by continuing.

4. Lack purpose and a plan.

Another characteristic of discouragement is inactivity. You seldom see a discouraged activist running to and fro trying to help others. When you are discouraged, you tend to withdraw.

Many times discouragement comes right after a successful venture. Elijah found this to be true. Perhaps he needed another Mt. Carmel to lift his spirits. When we lack a purpose, many times we lack fulfillment.

By this time you may be totally discouraged, thinking there is little you can do to overcome those feelings of frustration and inadequacy. But here are some steps you can take.

1. POSITIVE ACTION

Take action on the problem. The moment you are certain of the source of the discouragement, get busy. Nothing delivers us from discouragement quicker than taking positive steps to solve the problem.

2. POSITIVE THINKING

Years ago I read a brief but stimulating biography of Thomas Edison written by his son. What an amazing character! Thanks to his genius, we enjoy the microphone, the phonograph, the incandescent light, the storage battery, talking movies, and more than a thousand other inventions. But beyond all that, Edison was a man who refused to be discouraged. His contagious optimism affected all those around him.

His son recalled a freezing December night in 1914. Unfruitful experiments on the nickel-iron-alkaline storage battery, a ten-year project, had put Edison on a financial tightrope. He was still solvent only because of profits from movie and record production.

On that December evening, the cry "Fire!" echoed through the plant. Spontaneous combustion had broken out in the film room. Within minutes all the packing compounds, celluloid for records and film, and other flammable goods were burning. Fire companies from eight surrounding towns arrived, but the heat was so intense and the water pressure so low that attempts to douse the flames were futile. Everything was being destroyed.

When he couldn't find his father, the son became concerned. Was he safe? With all his assets being destroyed, would his spirit be broken? Soon he saw his father in the plant yard running toward him.

"Where's Mom?" shouted the inventor. "Go get her, Son! Tell her to hurry up and bring her friends! They'll never see a fire like this again!"

Early the next morning, long before dawn, with the fire barely under control, Edison called his employees together and made an incredible announcement. "We're rebuilding!"

He told one man to lease all the machine ships in the area. He told another to obtain a wrecking crane from the Erie Railroad Company. Then, almost as an afterthought, he added, "Oh, by the way, anybody here know where we can get some money?"

Later he explained, "We can always make capital out of a disaster. We've just cleared out a bunch of old rubbish. We'll build bigger and better on the ruins." Shortly after that, he yawned, rolled up his coat for a pillow, curled up on a table, and immediately fell asleep.[1]

3. Positive Example

It happened in Southwest Asia in the fourteenth century. The army of Asian conqueror Emperor Tamerlane (a descendant of Genghis Khan) had been routed, dispersed by a powerful enemy. Tamerlane himself lay hidden in a deserted manger while enemy troops scoured the countryside.

As he lay there, desperate and dejected, Tamerlane watched an ant try to carry a grain of corn over a perpendicular wall. The kernel was larger than the ant itself. As the emperor counted, sixty-nine times the ant tried to carry it up the wall. Sixty-nine times he fell back. On the seventieth try he pushed the grain of corn over the top.

Tamerlane leaped to his feet with a shout! He, too, would

triumph in the end! And he did, reorganizing his forces and putting the enemy to flight.

4. POSITIVE PERSISTENCE

Too many times we become discouraged and accept defeat. One of the most famous race horses of all time was Man o' War. As a two-year-old, Man o' War won six consecutive races. Then in 1919, the champ came across a contender appropriately named Upset. For the first time in his life, Man o' War trailed another horse across the finish line.

As is often the case when a champion goes down in defeat, there were the usual circumstances that affected the situation. On this occasion, an assistant starter was working the gate at the Saratoga race track, and the break from the barrier was delayed for about five minutes. The champ, always nervous at the post, was dancing and bobbing his head, and when the field broke, the big red horse was off sideways, fifth in a seven-horse race.

A champion does not give up easily, and Man o' War was no exception. He made a gallant try to close the gap. Given another two or three lengths, Man o' War would have been a clear winner, but Upset won by the narrowest possible margin.

When you read about that incident, you wish that the upset by Upset would have never happened.

You wish, too, that upsets some great people have experienced would have never happened either. Abraham failed in an hour of emergency, and in weakness let a king think his wife, Sarah, was his sister. There is Jacob, who tricked his brother out of his own birthright; Moses, whose impatience lost him the right to enter the promised land; and David, that "man after God's own heart" (Sam. 13:14), who tarnished his name through adultery and murder. Elijah, too, was upset and prayed to die.

But—and this is what is most important of all—all these

men, after tragic upsets, went on to win great victories (as did Man o' War one year later when he upset Upset).

Has some upsetting defeat or discouragement come your way recently? It's up to you to decide how you will handle the defeats of life. No one will go through all of life without meeting defeat from time to time. When it happens to you, don't quit! Missionary E. Stanley Jones said that he had adopted as his motto for life, "When life kicks you, let it kick you forward!" A wise resolve! Anyone can start, but only a thoroughbred will finish.

—————— Attitude Application ——————

Harold Sherman, quite awhile ago, wrote a book entitled *How to Turn Failure into Success*.[2] In it he gives a "Code of Persistence." If you tend to give up too easily, write this down and read it daily:

1. I will never give up so long as I know I am right.
2. I will believe that all things will work out for me if I hang on until the end.
3. I will be courageous and undismayed in the face of odds.
4. I will not permit anyone to intimidate me or deter me from my goals.
5. I will fight to overcome all physical handicaps and setbacks.
6. I will try again and again and yet again to accomplish what I desire.
7. I will take new faith and resolution from the knowledge that all successful men and women have had to fight defeat and adversity.
8. I will never surrender to discouragement or despair no matter what seeming obstacles may confront me.

THE STRUGGLE OF SIN

The third storm that rages within and causes our attitude to crash is: the *struggle of sin.*

> For that which I am doing, I do not understand; for I am not practicing what I would like to do, but I am doing the very thing I hate. But if I do the very thing I do not wish to do, I agree with the Law, confessing that it is good. So now, no longer am I the one doing it, but sin which indwells me. For I know that nothing good dwells in me that is, in my flesh; for the wishing is present in me, but the doing of the good is not. For the good that I wish, I do not do; but I practice the very evil that I do not wish. But if I am doing the very thing I do not wish, I am no longer the one doing it, but sin which dwells in me. I find then the principle that evil is present in me, the one who wishes to do good. For I joyfully concur with the law of God in the inner man, but I see a different law in the members of my body, waging war against the law of my mind, and making me a prisoner of the law of sin which is in my members. Wretched man that I am! Who will set me free from the body of this death? Thanks be to God through Jesus Christ our Lord! So then, on the one hand I myself with my mind am serving the law of God, but on the other, with my flesh the law of sin (Rom. 7:15–25).

Paul is not a golfer describing his inconsistent game. Rather, he is writing about the conflict of two natures within him. One says, "Do good," while the other drags him down.

A new Christian was sharing with me his frustration over not always doing what was right and what he intended. This disciplined individual asked, "Pastor, do you understand what I feel?" My reply: "Yes, and so did Paul." I turned to Romans 7 and started reading. He stopped me and asked, "Where is that scripture? I will need to go back to it."

I hope he will also go to Romans 8 where Paul tells of deliverance. "There is therefore now no condemnation for those who are in Christ Jesus" (v. 1).

Susanna Wesley, mother of John and Charles, once used this striking sentence: "Whatever weakens your reason, impairs the tenderness of your conscience, obscures your sense of God, or removes your relish for spiritual things—that is sin to you."

Your attitude begins to falter when sin enters your life. A withdrawal, a hardness, and a fleshly nature begin to invade us, all caused by sin. It is first appealing, then appalling; first alluring, then alienating; first deceiving, then damning; it promises life and produces death; it is the most disappointing thing in the world.

Understanding the problem is a good first step in correcting your perspective. If your attitude is threatening to crash, check the internal indications. See if you are afraid of failure, dealing with discouragement, or struggling with sin.

10

❖❖❖

The Crash from Without

Internal problems are not the only things that endanger our perspective. Our attitude sometimes crashes when the storms around us begin to take their toll. I have pinpointed four of these outward causes.

The Closeness of Criticism

I call the first one the *closeness of criticism.*

I use the word *closeness* because the criticism that hurts always comes close to where we live or what we love. Others' criticism of us is like having someone "step on our blue suede shoes."

When speaking on this subject, many times I ask the audience if they can remember a critical statement that greatly affected their lives. I usually receive a unanimous "Yes."

I, too, have heard my share of critical comments. I grew up in a denomination that placed a high status on pastors who received yearly unanimous votes of confidence from their congregations. Conversation during summer church conferences centered on the most recent votes. This emphasis was firmly implanted in my mind, and my prayer for my first pastorate was, "Oh Lord, help me to please everybody." (That is definitely a prayer for failure.)

I did my best. I kissed the babies, visited the elderly, married the young, buried the dead, everything I thought I should do. Finally the annual vote was to be taken on my performance. Years later I still remember the results. Thirty-one yes, one no, and one abstention. Now what would you do? Not everyone was pleased with me. I rushed to the phone and called my father for his advice. Fortunately, he reassured me that the church would make it through the "crisis." Unfortunately, for six months I wondered who voted "no."

From that early pastoral experience, I learned the negative effect that criticism can have on a young church leader. A person entering his calling with a dream can easily be crushed unless he understands that the best fruit is the one the birds pick.

Jesus, perfect in love and motives, was criticized and misunderstood continually. People

- called Him a glutton (Matt. 11:19);
- called Him a drunkard (Luke 7:34);
- criticized Him for associating with sinners (Matt. 9:11); and
- accused Him of being a Samaritan and of having a demon (John 8:48).

In spite of experiencing misunderstanding, ingratitude, and rejection, our Lord never became bitter, discouraged, or overcome. Every obstacle was an opportunity. Brokenheartedness? An opportunity to comfort. Disease? An opportunity to heal. Hatred? An opportunity to love. Temptation? An opportunity to overcome. Sin? An opportunity to forgive. Jesus turned trials into triumphs.

We always hurt ourselves when our reactions toward those who criticize us become negative. When such feelings arise, it is important to read the teachings of Jesus:

> You have heard that it was said, "YOU SHALL LOVE YOUR NEIGHBOR, and hate your enemy." But I say to you, love your enemies, and pray for those who persecute you in order that you may be sons of your Father who is in heaven; for He causes the sun to rise on the evil and the good, and sends rain on the righteous and the unrighteous. For if you love those who love you, what reward have you? Do not even the tax-gatherers do the same? And if you greet brothers only, what do you do more than others? Do not even the Gentiles do the same? Therefore you are to be perfect, as your heavenly Father is perfect. (Matt. 5:43–48)

Attitude Application

Here are some ways to keep criticism from sabotaging your attitude:

1. When possible, avoid people who belittle you. Small people try to tear you down, but big people make you feel worthwhile.
2. Ask yourself: What bothers me most when I am criticized? Who said it? Why was it said? What was the attitude that accompanied it? The place where it was shared? Is criticism coming from different people about the same subject? Is it valid? If so, am I doing anything about it?
3. Find a friend who has the gift of encouragement. Go to him and receive healing from his gift. But never

receive his support without using your gift to minister in return.

The Presence of Problems

The second storm is the *presence of problems.*

Life is full of problems, and we might as well be prepared for them. There is no such place as a trouble-free area and no such person as one who knows no problems. And Christians aren't exempt!

It is my responsibility and joy to disciple the key leaders of my congregation. A few years ago, we studied 2 Timothy in a series I call "Time Out for Timothy." One subject was "Persecution of the Christian Leader." The central thought: "All who desire to live godly lives in Christ Jesus will be persecuted." The major question discussed in this study was, "Can you name a Bible character greatly used of God who did not endure trials?" Take a moment to try it. Almost without exception, the people we read about in God's Word encountered troubles.

> When Noah ailed the waters blue
> He had his troubles same as you;
> For forty days he drove the ark
> Before he found a place to park.

At times we all become "flooded" with problems. Perhaps it is the number of difficulties more than the size of any one trouble that wears us down. We all have moments when we bite off more than we can chew.

When our attitude crashes, we have two alternatives. We can either alter the difficulty or alter ourselves. What can be changed for the best, we must change. When that is impossible, we must adjust to the circumstances in a positive way.

Before the days of antibiotics, Robert Louis Stevenson, the

great Scottish novelist and author of *Treasure Island*, was bedridden with consumption a great deal. But the disease never stifled his optimism. Once when his wife heard him coughing badly, she said to him, "I expect you still believe it's a wonderful day."

Stevenson looked at the rays of sunshine bouncing off the walls of his bedroom, then replied, "I do. I will never permit a row of medicine bottles to block my horizon."[1]

The apostle Paul possessed the same attitude. He said:

We are pressed on every side by troubles, but not crushed and broken. We are perplexed because we don't know why things happen as they do, but we don't give up and quit. We are hunted down, but God never abandons us. We get knocked down, but we get up again and keep going (2 Cor. 4:8–9 TLB).

——— Attitude Application ———

What are the problems?

Predictors—They help mold our future.

Reminders—We are not self-sufficient. We need God and others to help.

Opportunities—They pull us out of our rut and cause us to think creatively.

Blessings—They open up doors that we usually do not go through.

Lessons—Each new challenge will be our teacher.

Everywhere—No place or person is excluded from them.

Messages—They warn us about potential disaster.

Solvable—No problem is without a solution.

THE CONFLICT OF CHANGE

The third external storm that can cause our attitude to fall is the *conflict of change*.

We resist nothing more than change. Many times we enjoy the rewards of change but endure its process. We are creatures of habit. We first form habits, then our habits form us. We are what we repeatedly do. It is easy to see our world only from our perspective. When that occurs, we stagnate and become narrow.

Read the following statements. One is always true. The other is not.

"Change brings growth."

"Growth brings change."

The first statement, "Change brings growth," is true only if your attitude is right. With the proper attitude, all change, whether positive or negative, will be a learning experience that results in a growing experience. Our inability to control changing situations has caused many attitudes to crash. Yet this does not have to happen. One Christmas I was walking through Skyline's offices wishing everyone a merry Christmas. Stopping to speak to one of the volunteer assistants, I asked, "Are you ready for Christmas?" With a smile she replied, "Almost. Just one more Care Bear to stuff." Figuring she was making the bears for her grandchildren, I asked, "How many grandchildren do you have?" "None," she replied. "But that's okay. I went out into my neighborhood and adopted some. I figured that if I'm going to have a family at Christmas, then I'd better go round them up!"

With a little coaxing from me, she began to explain some of the problems she'd had with her own family. The more she told me, the more I sensed that this remarkable lady refused to wallow in the pool of pity in which so many are drowning. Christmas to her would be lovely and not lonely only because she would not allow her attitude to crash over things she could not control.

Sadly, too many people are like the old man in northern Maine who had turned one hundred. A New York reporter who went up to interview him commented, "I'll bet you have seen lots of changes in your one hundred years."

The elderly fellow crossed his arms, jutted his jaw, and replied with indignation, "Yes, and I've been agin' every one of them!"

I have spent much time observing why and when people start resisting change. Some strive until they are comfortable, then they settle in and don't want to grow. For most, a negative experience has made them pull back and say "never again."

If they only knew how unhealthy such an attitude can be.

Change is essential for growth. A famous inventor once said, "The world hates change, yet it is the only thing that has brought progress." Even when people realize that change is inevitable, they respond differently to its challenges. Some retreat into their emotional and spiritual bomb shelters and refuse to become a part of the action. One church member said to his pastor, "It's such a relief to come to a church where nothing has changed in thirty years!" My heart bleeds for that pastor.

On the other hand, there are those who go to the other extreme and change with every new gust of wind. They jump from bandwagon to bandwagon, and they are always looking for some new thing. The old hymns are buried, the familiar forms of worship are laid to rest, and even the traditional terminology is replaced by a jargon that may leave the poor worshiper wondering whether even God understands what is going on.

Still, the right amount of change can strengthen us. Moses uses an interesting illustration in Deuteronomy 32:11, where he describes the mother eagle forcing her young to leave the nest and fly. The eaglet wants to stay in the nest and be fed, but if he remains there, he will never use his great wings or enjoy the great heights for which he was created. So his mother has to knock him out of the nest, catch him on her wings when he falls too far, and repeat the process until he learns to fly on his own.

You and I enjoy our little nests, and we have worked hard to build them. This explains why we resent it when God starts to "shake up" the nest. God wants us to grow. The timid souls pray, "Oh, that I had wings like a dove! I would fly away and be at rest" (Ps. 55:6). But the courageous should claim Isaiah 40:31 and "mount up with wings as eagles" right in the face of the wind! Not everybody who grows old grows up, and those who fail to grow up are often the ones who have run away from the challenge of change.

THE NIGHT OF NEGATIVISM

The fourth storm, which causes more attitude fatalities than anything else, is what I call the *night of negativism*.

Our thoughts govern our actions. That is a fact. In Matthew 15:19, the Lord said, "For out of the heart come evil thoughts, murders, adulteries, fornications, thefts, false witness, slander." The question is, are we governed by negative or positive thoughts? As negative thoughts produce negative actions, so positive thoughts produce positive actions. Today we are where we are and what we are because of the thoughts that dominate our minds.

Our challenge is to think right in a negative world. Negative thinking and living do many detrimental things to our lives. Let's look at a few of them.

1. NEGATIVE THINKING CREATES CLOUDS AT CRITICAL DECISION TIMES.

We become tense instead of relaxing. Taking a test is an example of this. An often-heard comment while cramming is, "I hope they don't ask me that question. I'm sure I'll miss it." We start the test, and sure enough, there is the question, followed by the predicted outcome. Accident? No. It's a prophecy fulfilled. You felt negative about the question, declared your fear, and responded accordingly. Next time you're studying for an exam, say to yourself, "If there ever will be a time when I remember the answer to this question, it will be when I take the test."

2. Negative talking is contagious.

A man who lived by the side of the road and sold hot dogs was hard of hearing, so he had no radio. He had trouble with his eyes, so he read no newspapers. But he sold good hot dogs. He put up signs on the highway advertising them. He stood on the side of the road and cried, "Buy a hot dog, mister?" And people bought his hot dogs. He increased his meat and bun orders. He bought a bigger stove to take care of his trade.

He finally got his son to come home from college to help out. But then something happened. "Father, haven't you been listening to the radio?" his son said. "Haven't you been reading the newspaper? There's a big recession on. The European situation is terrible. The domestic situation is worse."

Whereupon the father thought, *Well, my son's been to college, he reads the papers, and he listens to the radio, and he ought to know.*

So the father cut down his meat and bun orders, took down his signs, and no longer bothered to stand out on the highway to sell his hot dogs. His sales fell overnight.

"You're right, son," the father said to the boy. "We certainly are in the middle of a big recession."

Has someone else's negative attitude ever changed your actions?

3. Negative thinking blows everything out of proportion.

Some people treat the drip from a leaky roof like a hurricane. Everything is a major project. They find a problem in every solution.

Murphy's Law states, "Nothing is as easy as it looks; everything takes longer than you expect; and if anything can go wrong, it will and at the worst possible moment."

Maxwell's Law states, "Nothing is as hard as it looks; everything is more rewarding than you expect; and if anything can go right, it will and at the best possible moment."

4. NEGATIVE THINKING LIMITS GOD AND OUR POTENTIAL.

One of the saddest stories in the Bible is about Israel's failure to enter the promised land as told in Numbers 13 and 14. It is a classic example of how a negative report can limit God and others.

Twelve spies went into Canaan under the same orders, to the same places, at the same time, and came back with different advice. For Joshua and Caleb, the promised land was everything that God said it would be. They reported, "It certainly does flow with milk and honey, and this is its fruit" (Num. 13:27).

The other ten men offered a negative report. In verses 28 and 29 of chapter 13, they reported facts without faith:

> Nevertheless, the people who live in the land are strong, and the cities are fortified and very large; and moreover, we saw the descendants of Anak there. Amalek is living in the land of the Negev and the Hittites and the Jebusites and the Amorites are living in the hill country, and the Canaanites are living by the sea and by the side of the Jordan.

In verse 31 we see that they have goals without God: "But the men who had gone up with them said, 'We are not able to go up against the people, for they are too strong for us.'"

Verses 32 and 33 tell us that they continued with exaggeration without encouragement:

So they gave out to the sons of Israel a bad report of the land which they had spied out, saying, "The land through which we have gone, in spying it out, is a land that devours its inhabitants; and all the people whom we saw in it are men of great size. There also we saw Nephilim (the sons of Anak are part of the Nephilim); and we became like grasshoppers in our own sight, and so we were in their sight."

The result?

Then all the congregation lifted up their voices and cried, and the people wept that night. And all the sons of Israel grumbled against Moses and Aaron; and the whole congregation said to them, "Would that we had died in the land of Egypt! Or would that we had died in the wilderness! And why is the LORD bringing us into this land, to fall by the sword? Our wives and our little ones will become plunder; would it not be better for us to return to Egypt?" So they said to one another, "Let us appoint a leader and return to Egypt." (Num. 14:1–4)

They settled for second best.

5. NEGATIVE THINKING KEEPS US FROM ENJOYING LIFE.

A negative person expects nothing off a silver platter except tarnish. If you have a negative neighbor, borrow a cup of sugar from him. He never expects to be paid back. Chisolm, a thinker and the "father of this crowd," said, "Any time things appear to be getting better, you have overlooked something."

6. NEGATIVE THINKING HINDERS OTHERS FROM MAKING A POSITIVE RESPONSE.

This is probably the greatest danger of a negative lifestyle. It tends to control those you influence and love the most.

Even the answer to a question depends a great deal on how you ask it. As experienced salespeople have long known, questions phrased either positively or negatively usually elicit a corresponding reply.

For example, a young psychology student drafted into the army decided to test this theory. Drawing KP, he was given the job of passing out apricots at the end of the chow line.

"You don't want apricots, do you?" he asked the first few men. Ninety percent said, "No."

Then he tried the positive approach. "You do want some apricots, don't you?" About half answered, "Uh, yeah, I'll take some."

Then he tried a third test, based on the fundamental either/or selling technique. "One dish of apricots or two," he asked. And in spite of the fact that most soldiers don't like army apricots, 40 percent took two dishes, and 50 percent took one.

The most common type of negativism that hinders others is characterized by what I call a "flat world" statement. This is a sincere statement that has been conditioned by past education and experience. It is not true, yet it is accepted as fact. Therefore it directs the thinking and action of many individuals.

History abounds with tales of experts who said positively that things could not be done—and were proven wrong. During the early 1900s an impressive array of scientific wizards pooh-poohed the idea of the airplane. Stuff and nonsense, they said. A crackpot idea.

One of America's influential scientific journalists hurried to say, "Time and money is being wasted on aircraft experimentation."

One week later, on a bumpy field in Kitty Hawk, North Carolina, the Wright Brothers taxied their crackpot idea down a homemade runway and launched the human race into the air.

Even after that, the experts continued to snipe at the airplane.

Marshall Foch, Supreme Commander of the Allied Forces in France in World War I, watched a display and said, "All very well for sport, but it is no use whatsoever to the army."

Thomas Edison is on record as having said that talking pictures would never catch on. "Nobody," he said, "would pay to listen to sounds coming from a screen."

He also tried to persuade Henry Ford to abandon his work on the fledgling idea of a motor car. "It's a worthless idea," Edison, persistent in his own endeavors, told the young Ford. "Come and work for me and do something really worthwhile."

Benjamin Franklin was told by experts to stop all that foolish experimenting with lightning. It was a waste of time, they said.

Today we are still having difficulty with "flat world" people. Many of our accepted assumptions have a tendency to stifle creativity and the achievement of our true potential.

To crystalize our understanding of this subtle form of negativism, I have listed some "flat world" statements:

"Leaders are born, not made."
"Nice guys finish last."
"It's not what you know, it's who you know."
"You can't teach an old dog new tricks."

When we become conditioned to perceived truths and closed to new positive possibilities, the following happens:

We *see* what we *expect* to see, not what we *can* see.
We *hear* what we *expect* to hear, not what we *can* hear.
We *think* what we *expect* to think, not what we *can* think.

———— Attitude Application ————

How do you make your "flat world" round?

1. Identify the reason you are a "flat world" person.
2. Identify the areas in which you think "flat world."
3. Identify people who can help you change this limiting thought process.
4. Continually check up on your progress.
5. Read and listen to positive self-help books and tapes.
6. Accept very few dogmatic, extreme statements.
7. Place all statements made into their proper context.
8. Take into account the source of the statement.
9. Remember, experience can limit your perspective rather than expand it.
10. What is possible is not always achieved quickly and endorsed enthusiastically.

Closing thought:

A "flat world" mind-set allows us to sleep on top of it.
A "round world" mind-set keeps us moving around it.

THE CHANGING OF YOUR ATTITUDE

11

Up, Up, and Away

One of the great discoveries we make, one of our great surprises, is to find we can do what we were afraid we couldn't do. Most of the prison bars we beat against are within us; we put them there, and we can take them down.

Now, that statement includes some good news and some bad news. The bad news is that we bring many of our problems on ourselves. The good news is that beginning today, we can break out of our prison of bad attitudes and become free for effective living.

This section is dedicated to clearly laying out a workable process to help you overcome an attitude problem. For this process to be successful, you should understand these statements:

1. The process takes a lot of dedication and work to be effective.
2. The process of change is never complete; therefore, constant review of section IV will ensure the best results.
3. All excuses for wrong attitudes must be eliminated immediately. Face changing with the sincerity and honesty of the old hymn that says, "It's me, it's me, it's me, oh, Lord, standing in the need of prayer."
4. Find a friend to whom you can be accountable on a regular basis for your change of attitude.
5. Remember, as you read these next pages, you are able to change any attitude you desire.

The individual's attitude is my major emphasis in speaking around the world. Most people are very close to becoming the person God wants them to be. Continually I say to them and now to you, "You're only an attitude away!" My greatest joy is in helping hundreds of people change an attitude they feel stuck with for the rest of their lives. For your encouragement, I've included in this chapter a testimonial of a changed life resulting from a changed attitude. Read this person's story and remember, this can happen to you:

"As a man thinks within himself, so he is" (Prov. 23:7). This verse has special significance for me. I have personally experienced the influence of attitudes, for my thinking in life has produced two different men.

My conversion to Christ was the turning point for me. I changed from being a person with negative attitudes to one who lives with a positive mind-set. People see me as a very positive person today, but they would not have recognized me eleven years ago. My attitudes have come through a healing, reshaping, transforming process.

Before I was a Christian, my attitude was shaped by the world around me. My thinking was conformed to the world's values. I was reared in a broken home and was saturated with the attitude that life was a struggle, a fight for survival. I had a negative self-image because the significant people in my life (family, peers, etc.) possessed negative self-images. Criticism and negative thinking became my way of life because those attitudes were modeled by the people around me. Obstacles and problems were curses to be lived with, not blessings in disguise that could be solved.

I felt that life had dealt me a bad hand. I was doomed to have the "short end of the stick." I became self-centered and self-seeking. I wanted only to see what I could get from life. As I pursued this negative lifestyle, I found no fulfillment. Life itself seemed meaningless; it always had a dark cloud hanging over it.

The people I associated with, the literature I read, the music I listened to, and my failure to know God all shaped my attitudes in a non-positive way.

Christ came into my life at a very significant point. When I was most discouraged with living, He made me a new person. I began to see that "Christ in me" meant a transformation of my mind. I did not become a super-positive person overnight, but I began immediately to see life differently.

His Word within me, not the world around me, began to influence my attitudes. I made a willful choice to abide by God's Word. I had a battle with recurring negative thoughts. But I desired with all my heart to be different. I wanted to be a positive person. I wanted to have the mind of Christ.

As I learned more about Christ, submitted to His will,

and obeyed His leading, my bitterness toward life changed. Life became a blessing, not a burden. Life was full of opportunities, not obstacles.

I purposely set out to expose myself to positive role models. I read positive-thinking books, listened to positive people, associated with positive groups. Please be aware that these changes were not always easy. I had to battle the old thinking sometimes. But the grace of God was the key factor in transforming my attitude.

Certainly this man has undergone some tremendous changes. Every time I read his personal testimony, I sense much positive growth in his life. Fortunately he is a close friend, and I have been able to see the success of his new, positive attitude. When change is successful, we look back and call it growth.

Most people who have negative attitudes do not realize that attitudes know no barriers. The only barriers that bring our attitudes into bondage are those we place upon them. Attitudes, like faith, hope, and love, can cross over any obstacle. Realizing this truth, let me encourage you to take control of your attitudes and begin the needed changes.

12

The Choice Within You

We are either the masters or the victims of our attitudes. It is a matter of personal choice. Who we are today is the result of choices we made yesterday. Tomorrow we will become what we choose today. To change means to choose to change.

Please follow carefully the course that you chart for your change of attitude. Down the road you'll be glad you did. Only you can determine to take the first steps that must be taken, but they are also the most important. Without taking these, it will be impossible to take the others.

Choice #1—Evaluate your present attitudes.

This will take some time. If possible, try to separate yourself from your attitudes. The goal of this exercise is not to see the "bad you" but the "bad attitude" that keeps you from being a more fulfilled person. This evaluation helps you make key changes only when you identify the problem.

Results are the only real reason for activity. The following evaluation process is developed to help you search for the right answers in the most efficient way.

Stages of Evaluation

1. Identify problem feelings—What attitudes make you feel the most negative about yourself? Usually feelings can be sensed before the problem is clarified. Write them down.

2. Identify problem behavior—What attitudes cause you the most problems when dealing with others? Write them down.

3. Identify problem thinking—We are the sum of our thoughts. "As a man thinks within himself, so he is." What thoughts consistently control your mind? Although this is the beginning step in correcting attitude problems, these are not as easy to identify as the first two.

4. Clarify biblical thinking—What do the Scriptures teach about you as a person and about your attitudes? Later in this section I will share a scriptural view of right attitudes.

5. Secure commitment—"What must I do to change?" now becomes "I must change." Remember, the choice to change is the one decision that must be made, and only you can make it.

6. Plan and carry out your choice—This is the process that section IV helps you accomplish.

Suggestion: This evaluation will take time. If you have an encouraging friend who knows you well, perhaps you should enlist his or her help.

CHOICE #2—REALIZE THAT FAITH IS STRONGER THAN FEAR.

The only thing that will guarantee the success of a doubtful undertaking is the faith from the beginning that you can do it. Jesus said, "If you have faith, and do not doubt, you shall . . . say it to this mountain, 'Be taken up and cast into the sea,' and it shall happen" (Matt. 21:21).

There is a biblical way to handle fear so that an endeavor can be successful and not be limited by it. The early church in Acts was experiencing tremendous growth. However, in Acts 4, Christians came up against some stiff opposition. They were commanded to stop witnessing or suffer severe consequences. Together they withdrew to pray. Verses 29 to 31 record a process they underwent to handle their fear. As you approach changing attitudes, this formula for fear will be helpful.

FOUR-STEP FORMULA TO HANDLE FEAR
1. Understand that God sees your problems.

"And now, Lord, take note of their threats . . ." (v. 29).

These who encountered difficulties wanted the assurance that God had seen their persecution. When things are going well, we do not need constant assurance that God is with us. But during battle (and you will have battles), there is a strong need for security. The good news is God Himself has said, "I WILL NEVER DESERT YOU, NOR WILL I EVER FORSAKE YOU" (Heb.13:5).

2. Ask for a filling of confidence and love that is greater than fear.

"Grant that Your bond-servants may speak Your word with all confidence" (Acts 4:29).

This was a request for more positive things to fill their hearts and minds. They realized that an effective way to experience less fear was to have more courage. It is unrealistic to think that all apprehensions, questions, and intimidations will flee and never haunt us again. Usually both positive and negative are at work in our lives at the same time. The secret to overcoming? Possess positive emotions and seek positive reinforcements that are stronger than the negatives.

3. Believe God is working a miracle in your life.

". . . while You extend Your hand to heal, and signs and wonders take place through the name of Your holy servant Jesus" (v. 30).

Now there was a prayer for God to intercede on their behalf with miracles. They realized that what had to be done would take their effort plus God's. Notice they asked for strength first, and then they requested that God would make up the difference.

This must happen in your life. Place the changes you seek in attitude, thinking, and behavior at the top of your prayer list. Ask God to help you do what is possible to bring about effective change. Then ask Him to do for you what you cannot do for yourself.

4. Be filled with the Holy Spirit.

"And when they had prayed, the place where they had gathered together was shaken, and they were all filled with the Holy Spirit, and began to speak the word of God with boldness" (v. 31).

There is a definite relationship between the filling of the Holy Spirit and boldness. Later in this section, more emphasis will be given to the need for Spirit-filled living.

I know many people who use this four-step formula to handle fear on a daily basis. It guards them and imparts strength. I encourage you to continually refer to this formula when fears begin to hinder your progress.

You are now preparing to take a step. Don't be fearful or hesitant. You can't cross a chasm in two small jumps. The future is worth the risk. Tomorrow you will look back at the changes and call them improvements.

Years ago a small town in Maine was proposed for the site of a great hydroelectric plant. Since a dam would be built across the river, the town would be submerged. When the project was announced, the people were given many months to arrange their affairs and relocate.

During the time before the dam was built, an interesting thing happened. All improvements ceased. No painting was done. No repairs were made on the buildings, roads, and sidewalks. Day by day the whole town got shabbier and shabbier. A long time before the waters came, the town looked uncared for and abandoned, even though the people had not yet moved away. One citizen complained, "Where there is no faith in the future, there is no power in the present." That town was cursed with hopelessness because it had no future.

Choice #3—Write a statement of purpose.

When I was a boy, my father decided to build a basketball court for my brother and me. He made a cement driveway, put a backboard on the garage, and was just getting ready to put up the basket when he was called away on an emergency. He promised to put up the hoop as soon as he returned. *No problem,* I thought, *I have a brand-new Spalding ball and a new cement driveway on which to dribble it.* For a few minutes I bounced the ball on the cement. Soon that became boring, so I took the ball and threw it up against the backboard—once. I let the ball run off the court and didn't pick it up again until Dad returned to put up the rim. Why? It's no fun playing basketball without a goal. The joy is having something to aim for.

In order to have fun and direction in changing your attitude, you must establish a clearly stated goal. This goal should be as specific as possible, written out, and signed, with a time frame attached to it. The purpose statement should be placed in a visible spot where you see it several times a day to give you reinforcement. Here is an example of a statement of purpose:

"To change my attitude (specifically, negative thinking, critical remarks toward others, and resentment) by following the procedure outlined in section IV of this book. To effectively accomplish this goal I will review this process and my progress daily by being accountable to an encouraging friend. By (date) _____ I fully expect that others will be noticing my positive behavior."

You will attain this goal if each day you do three things:

1. Write specifically what you desire to accomplish each day.

The story of David's encounter with Goliath is a fine illustration of faith and how it may move against insurmountable odds with seemingly inadequate resources. But one thing perplexed me when I first began to study David's life. Why did he pick five stones for his sling on his way to encounter Goliath? There was only one giant. Choosing five stones seemed to be a flaw in his faith. Did he think he was going to miss and that he would have four more chances? Sometime later I was reading in 2 Samuel, and I got the answer. Goliath had four sons, so there were five giants. In David's reckoning, there was one stone per giant! Now that is what I mean about being specific in our faith.

What are the giants you must slay to make your attitude what it needs to be? What resources will you need? Don't be overcome with frustration when you see the problems. Take one giant at a time. Military strategists teach their armies to fight one front at a time. Settle which attitude you want to tackle at this time. Write it down. As you successfully begin to win battles, write them down. This will encourage you. Spend time reading about your past victories.

2. VERBALIZE TO YOUR ENCOURAGING FRIEND WHAT YOU WANT TO ACCOMPLISH EACH DAY.

Belief is inward conviction; faith is outward action. You will receive both encouragement and accountability by verbalizing your intentions. One of the ways people resolve a conflict is to verbalize it to themselves or someone else. This practice is also vital in reaching your desired attitudes.

I know successful salesperson who repeat this phrase out loud fifty times each morning and fifty times each evening: "I can do it." Continually saying and hearing these positive statements helps them believe in themselves and causes them to act on that belief. Start this process by changing your vocabulary. Here are some suggestions:

Eliminate These Words Completely	Make These Words a Part of Your Vocabulary
1. I can't	1. I can
2. If	2. I will
3. Doubt	3. Expect the best
4. I don't think	4. I know
5. I don't have the time	5. I will make the time
6. Maybe	6. Positively
7. I'm afraid of	7. I am confident
8. I don't believe	8. I do believe
9. (minimize) I	9. (promote) You
10. It's impossible	10. God is able

3. Take action on what you write, and verbalize what you wrote each day.

Jesus teaches us that the difference between a wise man and a foolish man is his response to what he already knows. A wise man follows up on what he hears while a foolish man knows but does not act (Matt. 7:24–27).

We are told in James 1:22–25:

> But prove yourself doers of the word, and not merely hearers who delude themselves. For if anyone is a hearer of the word and not a doer, he is like a man who looks at his natural face in a mirror; for once he has looked at himself and gone away, he has immediately forgotten what kind of a person he was. But one who looks intently at the perfect law, the law of liberty, and abides by it, not having become a forgetful hearer but an effectual doer, this man shall be blessed in what he does.

Choice #4—Have the desire to change.

No choice will determine the success of your attitude change more than desiring to change. When all else fails, desire alone can keep you heading in the right direction. Many people have climbed over insurmountable obstacles to make themselves better people when they realized that a change is possible if they really want it badly enough. Let me illustrate.

While hopping about one day, a frog happened to slip into a very large pothole along a country road. All his attempts at jumping out were in vain. Soon a rabbit came upon the frog trapped in the hole and offered to help him out. He, too, failed. After various animals from the forest made three or four gallant attempts to help the poor frog out, they finally gave up. "We'll go back and get you some food," they said. "It looks like you're going to be here awhile." However, not long after they took off to get food, they heard the frog hopping along after them. They couldn't believe it! "We thought you couldn't get out!" they exclaimed. "Oh, I couldn't," replied the frog. "But you see, there was a big truck coming right at me, and I had to."

It is when we "have to get out of the potholes of life" that we change. As long as we have acceptable options, we will not change. There seem to be three times in our lives when we're most receptive to change. First, when we hurt so much that we are forced to change. Jesus tells about this type of individual in Luke 15. The parable of the prodigal son illustrates that when we are looking up from the bottom of a pigpen, it is possible to come to ourselves and get help by going back to the father's house.

Second, receptivity to change is also heightened when we are bored and become restless. Everyone experiences this at certain times in life. Perhaps the parent senses this when the children are all in school and she finds extra time to get involved with other things. People plateau on their jobs and begin to lose interest in their work. A holy dissatisfaction can be healthy when it produces positive changes.

It is a sad day for any person when he becomes so satisfied with his life, his thoughts, and his deeds that he ceases to be challenged to do greater things in life.

Third, change is apt to occur when we realize we *can* change. This is the greatest motivation of all. Nothing sparks the fire of desire more than the sudden realization that you do not have to stay the same. You no longer need to feel the burden of negative attitudes. You have no valid reason to constantly feel bitter and resentful about life, others, or yourself. You can change!

Because I firmly believe that people will change once they understand that it is possible, I continually share one phrase with others. When I sense bewilderment, doubt, frustration, and other mental blocks, I say, "Yes, you can." I have seen hundreds of faces light up with those three simple words and an encouraging smile.

Life is a changing process. With all of its transitions come new opportunities for growth. What is a limiting factor yesterday may not be one today. Accept the following statement for your life: "The days ahead are filled with changes that are my challenges. I will respond to these opportunities with the confidence that my life will be better because of them. With God all things are possible."

Choice #5—Live one day at a time.

Anyone can fight the battle for just one day. It is only when you and I add the burdens of those two awful eternities, yesterday and tomorrow, that we tremble. It is not the experiences of today that drive men to distraction; it is the remorse or bitterness for something that happened yesterday and the dread of what tomorrow may bring. Let us therefore live but one day at a time—today!

David, in his prayer for forgiveness (Ps. 51), asked God to "hide Thy face from my sins" (v. 9). He understood that effectiveness today is determined by the healing and forgetting of yesterday. "My sin is ever before me" (v. 3) describes a condition in David's life that would have hindered the change he wanted to make. Therefore, he used words that pointedly asked God to spiritually heal his mind and heart. "Blot out my transgressions . . . wash me thoroughly . . . cleanse me from my sin . . . purify me . . . wash me . . . make me to hear joy and gladness . . . blot out all my iniquities . . . create in me a clean heart . . . renew a steadfast spirit within me . . . restore to me the joy of Thy salvation . . . deliver me" (vv. 1–2, 7–10, 12, 14).

Like David, you should pray these phrases and allow God to forgive you and heal your past. Only God can heal what happened yesterday and help you live effectively today. What you have not overcome in your past remains to plague you in your present.

CHOICE #6—CHANGE YOUR THOUGHT PATTERNS.

That which holds our attention determines our actions. We are where we are and what we are because of the dominating thoughts that occupy our minds. William James said, "The greatest discovery of my generation is that people can alter their lives by altering their attitudes of mind." Romans 12:1–2 says:

> I urge you therefore, brethren, by the mercies of God, to present your bodies a living and holy sacrifice, acceptable to God, which is your spiritual service of worship. And do not be conformed to this world, but be transformed by the renewing of your mind, that you may prove what the will of God is, that which is good and acceptable and perfect.

Two things must be stated to emphasize the power of our thought lives. Major premise: We can control our thoughts. Minor premise: Our feelings come from our thoughts. Conclusion? We can control our feelings by learning to change one thing: the way we think. It is that simple. Our feelings come from our thoughts. Therefore, we can change them by changing our thought patterns.

Our thought lives, not our circumstances, determine our happiness. Often I see people who are convinced that they will be happy when they attain a certain goal. When they reach the goal, many times they do not find the fulfillment they anticipated.

The secret to staying on an even keel? Fill your mind with "whatever is true, whatever is honorable . . . whatever is of good repute, if there is any excellence and if anything worthy of praise, let your mind dwell on these things" (Phil. 4:8). Paul understood. That which holds our attention determines our action.

Choice #7—Develop good habits.

Attitudes are nothing more than habits of thought. These cycle charts will help you form proper habits.

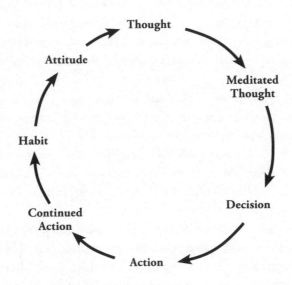

This cycle can be positive or negative. The process for developing habits, good or bad, is the same. It is as easy to form a habit of succeeding as it is to succumb to the habit of failure. Observe the following two cycles and see the difference.

Habits aren't instincts; they're acquired actions or reactions. They don't just happen; they are caused. Once the original cause of a habit is determined, it is within your power to accept or reject it. Most people allow their habits to control them. When those habits are hurtful, they damage our attitudes. The following formula will assist you in changing bad habits into good ones:

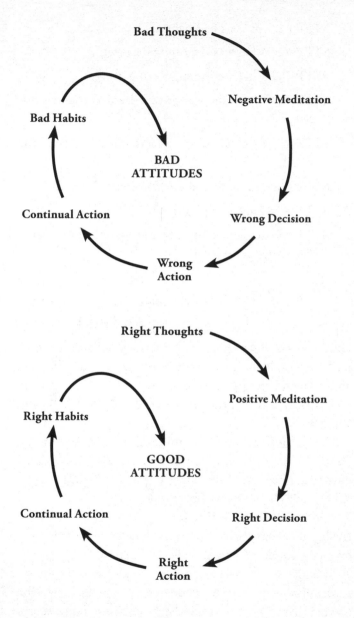

STEP #1: List your bad habits.

STEP #2: What was the original cause?

STEP #3: What are the supporting causes?

STEP #4: Determine a positive habit to replace the bad one.

STEP #5: Think about the good habit, its benefits and results.

STEP #6: Take action to develop this habit.

STEP #7: Daily act upon this habit for reinforcement.

STEP #8: Reward yourself by noting one of the benefits from your good habit.

Choice #8—Continually choose to have a right attitude.

Once you make the choice to possess a good attitude, the work really begins. Now comes a life of continually deciding to grow and maintain the right outlook. Attitudes have a tendency to revert back to their original patterns if not carefully guarded and cultivated.

"The hardest thing about milking cows," observed a farmer, "is that they never stay milked." Attitudes often don't stay changed. There are three stages of change in which you must deliberately choose the right attitude.

Early Stage—The first few days are always the most difficult. Old habits are hard to break. The mental process must be on guard continually to provide right action.

Middle Stage—The moment good habits begin to take root, options open that bring on new challenges. New habits are formed that will either be good or bad. The good news is: "Like begets like." The more right choices and habits you develop, the more likely good habits will be formed.

Late Stage—Complacency can become the enemy. We all know of incidents where someone (perhaps us) successfully lost weight, only to fall back into old eating habits and gain it back.

13

The Opportunities Around You

Once you have made the choice to change your attitude, you are ready to allow the opportunities around you to make this decision a success.

OPPORTUNITY #1—ENLIST THE COOPERATION OF A FRIEND.

We need one another. Few people are successful unless a lot of people want them to be. Change has a tendency to intimidate us. Add to that intimidation the realization that we have a long way to go before proper attitudes are established, and we begin to feel like the two cows grazing in a pasture that saw a milk truck pass. On the side of the truck were the words,

"Pasteurized, homogenized, standardized, Vitamin A added." One cow sighed and said to the other, "Makes you feel sort of inadequate, doesn't it?"

To help you overcome this feeling of inadequacy, you need the help of a friend. Find someone who has the spirit of Tenzing, the native guide of Edmund Hillary, who made the historic climb of Mt. Everest.

Coming down from the peak, Hillary suddenly lost his footing. Tenzing held the line taut and kept them both from falling by digging his ax into the ice. Later Tenzing refused any kind of special credit for saving Hillary's life; he considered it a routine part of the job. As he put it, "Mountain climbers always help each other."[1]

Tenzing realized that we can never do anything for others that will not have some eventual benefits for ourselves. There is a law of life that will, in time, return good for good. Therefore, enlisting someone's help will not only assist you, but it will also give a friend a blessing in return.

Conditions needed for successful, cooperative effort:

1. A friend you can see or talk to daily.
2. Someone who loves you and is an encourager.
3. Someone with whom you have mutual honesty and transparency.
4. A person who is successful in overcoming problems.
5. Someone who has strong faith in God and believes in miracles.

The book of Acts opens with the excitement of the early church. In the midst of all the joy and growth we see a very significant situation—John and Peter together in ministry and fellowship. The reason? John was encouraging Peter. A few weeks previously, Peter had denied his Lord and wasn't doing particularly well. In fact, he wanted to return to fishing. John, the disciple of love, decided to make Peter his ministry. Acts 3 records the miraculous healing of the lame man, but there was another healing taking place in Peter's life, an inner healing, as John walked with him to the temple. Could it be that Peter's greatness was at least partially a result of John's acceptance? Go find a friend like John.

OPPORTUNITY #2—ASSOCIATE WITH THE RIGHT PEOPLE.

One morning I walked into my office at Skyline and saw the following note on top of my desk: "Good morning, Pastor Maxwell. There are two keys to determine who we are: (1) who we perceive ourselves to be and (2) who we associate with."

How true! Yet as I reflect on that note, I conclude that a large portion of our self-image (who we conceive ourselves to be) is determined by our friendships. Accepting attitudes are based many times on how important the attitude is in complementing or damaging the image we feel other people have of us.

Birds of a feather do flock together. From friends, we acquire many of our thoughts, mannerisms, and characteristics. Changing an attitude from negative to positive often requires changing friendships. It is no accident that kids with good grades run around with other kids with good grades. While counseling people facing a broken marriage, I have observed that often the couple's friends are having marriage problems.

Many times people blame circumstances for their problems. But usually it is the crowd we run with, not the circumstances we encounter, that makes the difference in our lives. Good circumstances with bad friends result in defeat. Bad circumstances with good friends result in victory.

Opportunity #3—Select a model to follow.

Communicators say that 90 percent of what we learn is visual, 9 percent is audio, and 1 percent comes through the other senses. Our dependence on the eyes to learn, no doubt, is at least partially a result of television in our culture. Visual messages last longer than those we just hear. You could select someone to follow who would give you a constant visualization of what you want to become. Making a single decision to alter an attitude is not enough. The vision of what you desire must be constantly before you. To achieve the kind of life you want, you must act, walk, talk, and conduct yourself as the ideal person that you visualize yourself to be. Gradually that old self will pass away and be replaced with the new one.

My attitudes come as a result of proper modeling by my parents. Usually while speaking at conferences and trying to help people with their attitudes, I give several illustrations from my home life. One couple who listened to these illustrations desperately wanted to change themselves and their children. They decided to invite my mom and dad into their home for a weekend. This time spent together was helpful. One day while my mother was gone, the hostess entered the guest room and began to pray, and she asked God to give her my mother's wisdom and positive strengths just as Elijah's mantle had fallen on the prophet Elisha.

Begin looking for someone to stretch your life. If no one seems to be available, ask God to send you a Christian with a winning attitude. Ask that individual to disciple you for a few months. Enjoy the experience of growth by example.

Opportunity #4—Learn from your mistakes.

The first instant an idea is conceived is a moment of decision. When an opportunity for growth is opened to you, what do you tell yourself? Will you grasp the chance with a tingle of excitement and say, "I can make it work!" or do you smother it by saying, "That's impractical . . . too difficult . . . I don't think it can be done"? In that moment, you choose between success and failure. You help to form a habit of either positive or negative thinking by what you tell yourself. So give your "better" self a chance to grow. Form the habit of positive reaction followed by positive action. We cannot cause the wind to blow the way we want, but we can adjust our sails so that they will take us where we want to go.

You cannot control all circumstances. You cannot always make right decisions that bring right results. But you can always learn from your mistakes. The following formula will assist you in making the most of your mistakes.

FORMULA FOR OVERCOMING FAILURE

1. Recognize

What is failure? Is it permanent? Is there a second chance? Complete this sentence by circling the correct phrase:

A person is a failure when
(a) he makes a mistake;
(b) he quits;
(c) someone thinks he is.

2. Review

Failure should be our teacher, not our undertaker. Failure is delay, not defeat. It is a temporary detour, not a dead-end street. A winner is big enough to admit his mistakes, smart enough to profit from them, and strong enough to correct them. The only difference between the unsuccessful person and the successful person is that the unsuccessful person is mistaken three times out of five.

3. Repress

Perhaps your own personal problems and hang-ups caused the failure. If so, begin to work immediately on self-discipline. If you are the problem, put yourself under control. Lord Nelson, England's famous naval hero, suffered from seasickness throughout his entire life. Yet the man who had destroyed Napoleon's fleet did not let illness interfere with his career. He not only learned to live with his personal weakness, but he also conquered it. Most of us have our own little seasicknesses too. For some it may be physical, for others psychological. Usually it's a private war carried on quietly within us. No one will pin a medal on us for winning it, but nothing can dim the satisfaction of knowing that we did not surrender.

4. Readjust

An eminent plastic surgeon told of a boy who lost his hand at the wrist. When he asked the lad about his handicap, the boy replied, "I don't have a handicap. I just don't have a right hand." The surgeon went on to discover that this boy was one of the leading scorers on his high school football team. It's not what you have lost but what you have left that counts.

5. Reenter

Mistakes mark the road to success. He who makes no mistakes makes no progress. Make sure you generate a reasonable number of mistakes. I know that comes naturally to some people, but too many people are so afraid of error that they make their lives rigid with checks and counterchecks, discourage change, and in the end, so structure themselves that they will miss the kind of offbeat opportunity that can send their lives skyrocketing. So take a look at your record, and if you come to the end of a year and see that you haven't made many mistakes, ask yourself if you have tried everything you should have.

OPPORTUNITY #5—EXPOSE YOURSELF TO SUCCESSFUL EXPERIENCES.

It takes five positive experiences to overcome one negative situation. When faced with the possibility of failure, our tendency is to sit back and be anxious. Fear is nature's warning signal to get busy. We overcome it by successful action.

I once heard a speaker say, "We overcome by action." That is only partially true. Experiences that are continually unsuccessful can increase our desire to sit out the game in the arena of life. Action that produces confidence and a degree of success will encourage us to attempt new challenges.

I learned this when I played basketball in high school. One year our coach had a "brilliant" idea that would help us shoot our foul shots with greater accuracy. He replaced the regulation basketball rim with one that was smaller. He thought that if we could hit the smaller basket, it would be a cinch for us to make the larger one in the game. I watched my teammates practice foul shooting on the smaller rim. They missed frequently and seemed frustrated. Since I was captain of the team and an 80 percent shot from the foul line, I decided to approach my coach cautiously. My theory was opposite his. It was my belief that continually missing foul shots on the smaller rim would create an image of failure and result in missed shots in a game. That was exactly the result! Thinking back on that incident makes me wonder what would have happened if the coach had placed larger rims up on the backboard.

Nothing intimidates us more than constant exposure to failure. Nothing motivates us more than constant exposure to success. Therefore, I have found that people change more quickly if they are continually given situations in which they can be successful. Believing this, I set out to teach my daughter Elizabeth how to hit a ball with the bat. I didn't want her to stop swinging just because she might miss, because that would have given her a sense of failure, so I gave her the following instructions: "Elizabeth, it is your responsibility to swing the bat. It is my job to hit the bat with the ball when I pitch it."

Elizabeth fearlessly began to swing the bat. She had nothing to lose! Every time she would swing the bat, she was a success. The problem—I kept missing the bat with the ball I was throwing. Finally, after many swings and as many misses, Elizabeth threw down the bat, looked at me with disgust, and said, "Daddy, you keep missing the bat!"

Start exposing yourself today to successful people and experiences. Read books that will make you a better person. Find something that you can do well and do it often. Help make someone who needs your spiritual gifts a better person. Feed your right attitudes, and before you know it, your bad ones will starve to death. Write down your successes and review them often. Share your growth with those who are interested in you and already have excellent attitudes. Take time daily to congratulate yourself and thank others for making this change of attitude possible.

14

The God Above You

E. Stanley Jones made an impressive point when he said, "Anything less than God will let you down." And he went on to explain, "Anything less than God is not rooted in eternal reality. It has built-in failure." For every possible predicament of man, there is a corresponding grace of God. In other words: For every particular human need, there is a particular supernatural resource. For every definite problem, there is a definite answer. For every hurt, there is a cure. For every weakness, there is a strength. For every confusion, there is guidance.

There are several ways that God supports and strengthens our lives while we change.

Strength #1—God's Word

When the truths of the Bible permeate our minds and hearts, our attitudes can only improve. His Word is filled with people who continually demonstrate that man's right relationship with God gives him a healthy mind-set. Paul is just one example.

"I wonder why it is," an Anglican bishop once pondered, "that everywhere the apostle Paul went they had a revolution, and everywhere I go they serve a cup of tea."

Today we live relatively easy lives. But the apostle Paul could hardly set foot in a city before a riot started. It seemed like Paul was always getting into trouble. During his first missionary journey, he was stoned and left for dead. During his second missionary journey, he eluded arrest on charges of turning the world upside down. Throughout his life, Paul experienced incredible hardships: imprisonment, flogging, beatings, lashings, shipwreck, destitution, exhaustion. Hardly the "victorious Christian life" we often visualize, wouldn't you say? But despite his intense hardships and sufferings, Paul consistently maintained an attitude of thankfulness and joy. They threw him in a prison. What did he do? Grumble and complain? No! He sang hymns of joy to God (Acts 16:25). They threw him into prison again. He encouraged others to "rejoice in the Lord always" (Phil. 4:4). Paul's dominant attitude, whatever his circumstance, was joy. Where did Paul's joy come from?

Perhaps we can gain insight into Paul's victorious life by reading his letter to the Romans. Chapter 8 gives us what I call "Belief Foundations for a Positive Christian Attitude."

First Foundation—"I am truly significant."

And we know that God causes all things to work together for good to those who love God, to those who are called according to His purpose. For whom He foreknew, He also predestined to become conformed to the image of His Son; that He might be the first-born among many brethren; and who He predestined, these He also called; and whom He called, these He also justified; and whom He justified, these He also glorified. (vv. 28–30)

My sense of significance grows upon realizing that I am "called according to His purpose" (v. 28); "predestined to become conformed to the image of His Son" (v. 29); "called . . . justified . . . glorified" (v. 30).

SECOND FOUNDATION—"I AM TRULY SECURE."

What then shall we say to these things? If God is for us, who is against us? He who did not spare His own Son, but delivered Him up for us all, how will He not also with Him freely give us all things? Who will bring a charge against God's elect? God is the one who justifies; who is the one who condemns? Christ Jesus is He who died, yes rather who was raised, who is at the right hand of God, who also intercedes for us. Who shall separate us from the love of Christ? Shall tribulation, or distress, or persecution, or famine, or nakedness, or peril, or sword? Just as it is written, "FOR THY SAKE WE ARE BEING PUT TO DEATH ALL DAY LONG; WE WERE CONSIDERED AS SHEEP TO BE SLAUGHTERED." But in all these things we overwhelmingly conquer through Him who loved us. For I am convinced that neither death nor life, nor angels, nor principalities, nor things present, nor things to come, nor powers, nor height, nor depth, nor any other created thing shall be able to separate us from the love of God, which is in Christ Jesus our Lord (vv. 31–39).

When I know that I am secure in Him, I can afford to take a risk in my life. Only the insecure cannot afford to risk failure. The secure can be honest about themselves. They can admit failure. They are able to seek help and try again. They can change.

Remember the words of God in Jeremiah: "Is anything too difficult for Me?" (32:27). The Bible, not Norman Vincent Peale, first said, "All things are possible to him who believes" (Mark 9:23). The Scriptures, not Robert L. Schuller, first said, "Everything you ask in prayer, believing, you shall receive" (Matt. 21:22). God's Word gives us encouragement and guidance to change our lives.

Strength #2—Prayer

Many outstanding prayers in the Bible were effective yet brief. Psalm 25:1–10 is a short, simple, and sincere prayer. And it is also successful. The Lord's Prayer consists of 56 words. (Compare that with the 26,911 words in a government order setting the price of cabbage.)

Psalm 25 describes a person who has chosen the right road yet has not found it always easy to walk. The path is lined with enemies who would like nothing better than to put the weaker to shame. The traveler is also plagued with internal doubts as he recalls previous wanderings and failures. What he must realize is that the road is too difficult to walk without the companionship and friendship of God.

The psalmist, troubled from without and within, has stopped for a moment on the way. He knows he cannot turn back but scarcely knows how to continue. Therefore, he prays that God will help him follow through on his decision to stay on the right road.

We learn five things from this man of prayer in verses 1–10:

1. HE KNOWS IN WHICH DIRECTION TO LOOK FOR HELP.

> To Thee, O LORD, I lift up my soul (v. 1).

The humanist looks only to available human resources. The Christian immediately looks to God. The praying man realizes that God's blessings are not optional. They are a necessity.

2. HE KNOWS IN WHOM TO TRUST.

> O my God, in Thee I trust,
> Do not let me be ashamed;
> Do not let my enemies exult over me.
> Indeed, none of those who wait for Thee will be
> ashamed;
> Those who deal treacherously without cause will be
> ashamed. (vv. 2–3)

An attitude of trust is the key to effective praying based on the character of God. The thrust of our trust must be God-ward.

3. HE KNOWS THE PURPOSE OF PRAYER.

> Make me know Thy ways, O LORD;
> Teach me Thy paths.
> Lead me in Thy truth and teach me.
> For Thou art the God of my salvation;
> For Thee I wait all the day. (vv. 4–5)

The purpose of prayer is to change. Richard Foster says:

To pray is to change. Prayer is the central avenue God uses to transform us. If we are unwilling to change, we will abandon prayer as a noticeable characteristic of our lives. The more we pray, the more we come to the heartbeat of God. Prayer starts the communication process between ourselves and God. All the options of life fall before us. At that point we will either forsake our prayer life and cease to grow, or we will pursue our prayer life and let Him change us. Either option is painful. To not grow in His likeness is to not enjoy His fullness. When this happens, the priorities of the world begin to fade away.[1]

When we pray, asking God to change a situation, He usually begins with us.

4. He knows the basis of prayer.

> Remember, O Lord, Thy compassion and Thy
>   lovingkindness,
> For they have been from old.
> Do not remember the sins of my youth or my
>   transgressions;
> According to Thy lovingkindness remember
>   Thou me,
> For Thy goodness' sake, O Lord (vv. 6–7).

The psalmist cannot approach God on the basis of his own greatness, so he comes "according to Thy lovingkindness." David's change was based on who God is, not what he does.

5. He knows the future of prayer.

> Good and upright is the Lord:
> Therefore He instructs sinners in the way.
> He leads the humble in justice,
> And He teaches the humble His way.

All the paths of the LORD are lovingkindness and
    truth
to those who keep His covenant and His
    testimonies (vv. 8–10).

The future is as solid as God's character. The faithfulness of God is based on His attributes, not your actions. Take those wrong attitudes to Him.

STRENGTH #3—THE HOLY SPIRIT

In the New Testament the Spirit is referred to nearly three hundred times. The one word with which He is constantly associated is *power*. Jesus in John 16:4–16 teaches clearly the need for the Helper in our lives. The disciples were insecure about their future. Jesus said:

> But these things I have spoken to you, that when their hour comes, you may remember that I told you of them. And these things I did not say to you at the beginning, because I was with you. But now I am going to Him who sent Me; and none of you asks Me, "Where are You going?" But because I have said these things to you, sorrow has filled your heart. But I tell you the truth, it is to your advantage that I go away; for if I do not go away, the Helper shall not come to you; but if I go, I will send Him to you. And He, when He comes, will convict the world concerning sin, and righteousness, and judgment; concerning sin because they do not believe in Me; and concerning righteousness, because I go to the Father, and you no longer behold Me; and concerning judgment, because the ruler of this world has been judged. I have many more things to say to you, but you cannot hear them now. But when He, the Spirit of truth, comes, He will guide you into

all the truth; for He will not speak on His own initiative, but whatever He hears, He will speak; and He will disclose to you what is to come. He shall glorify Me, for He shall take of Mine, and shall disclose it to you. All things that the Father has are Mine; therefore I said, that He takes of Mine, and will disclose it to you. A little while, and you will no longer behold Me; and again a little while, and you will see Me.

Jesus said it was "to our advantage" that He would leave so the "Helper" could be sent to us. "The Spirit of truth" will guide us and glorify Jesus. In Acts 1, we read that our Lord was ready to go back to the Father. Surrounded by a few followers, Jesus shared with them these last important words:

He commanded them not to leave Jerusalem, but to wait for what the Father had promised, "Which," He said, "you heard of from Me; for John baptized with water, but you shall be baptized with the Holy Spirit not many days from now." And so when they had come together, they were asking Him, saying, "Lord, is it at this time You are restoring the Kingdom to Israel?" He said to them, "It is not for you to know the times or epochs which the Father has fixed by His own authority; but you shall receive power when the Holy Spirit has come upon you; and you shall be My witnesses both in Jerusalem and in all Judea and Samaria, and even to the remotest part of the earth" (Acts 1:4–8).

Power was promised when the Holy Spirit was received. Until Pentecost, the disciples were at best a questionable crew. Of the original twelve, Judas was already gone. James and John certainly were to be questioned about their motives and political desires. Thomas continually doubted. And there was Peter—glorious one moment, gone the next. Declaring truths, then denying them. What were his plans after the death of Christ? He had fishing on his mind.

Jesus had spent three years with the disciples. They had listened to His teaching, yet they needed something more than learning. He had performed many miracles, yet they were frustrated with their inadequate human endeavors. Upon the disciples' request, Jesus taught them to pray, yet they lacked real power in their lives. The Lord's discipline still had not given His small group of followers the effectiveness they needed to begin the early church. Jesus knew what they needed. Therefore He encouraged them to wait for the filling of the Holy Spirit in their lives.

They waited, and they were filled. The early church was launched! The theme of this growing group of believers was "forward through the storm." Seven difficult problems confronted this New Testament church of the book of Acts. After each obstacle, we read that the church was enlarged and the Word of God multiplied. Setbacks became springboards. Obstacles were turned into opportunities. Barriers turned out to be blessings. Cowards became courageous. Why? Those within the church were filled with the Holy Spirit.

That same power can be given to you.

As you desire to change and act on your plans to change, remember you're not doing this by yourself. First John 4:4 says, "You are from God, little children, and have overcome them, because greater is He who is in you than he who is in the world."

You will experience that overcoming power as you remember this:

FORMULA FOR SPIRITUAL SUCCESS

If you want to be distressed—look within.
If you want to be defeated—look back.
If you want to be distracted—look around.
If you want to be dismayed—look ahead.
If you want to be delivered—look up!

Channels for Change

Daily review this chart. It is designed to

1. encourage you in your pursuit of change;
2. direct you so you won't lose momentum; and
3. fill you with the right information.

Remember: There is no improvement except through change.

I. The Choice Within You

Choice #1—Evaluate Your Present Attitudes (Phil. 2:5). Are my attitudes today pleasing Christ and me?

Choice #2—Think, Is Your Faith Stronger Than Fear (Matt. 21:21)? Am I taking faith-action on my present fears?

Choice #3—Write a Statement of Purpose (Phil. 3:13–14). Have I written, verbalized, and acted on a plan to change my attitude?

Choice #4—Determine If You Have the Desire to Change (Ps. 37:4). Change is possible *if* I want it badly enough. Am I willing to pay the price?

Choice #5—Live One Day at a Time (Matt. 6:34). Am I allowing tomorrow's troubles to sap me of today's strength?

Choice #6—Change Your Thought Patterns (Phil. 4:8). That which holds our attention determines our action. Am I thinking on the right things?

Choice #7—Develop Good Habits (Deut. 6:5–9). Am I repeatedly acting on positive habits to overcome negative ones?

Choice #8—Continually Choose the Right Attitude (Prov. 3:31). **Am I continually choosing to change?**

II. The Opportunities Around You

Opportunity #1—Enlist the Cooperation of a Good Friend (Deut. 32:30). **Do I meet regularly with a friend who helps me?**

Opportunity #2—Associate with the Right People (James 4:4). **Are my friends helping or hindering my changes?**

Opportunity #3—Select a Model to Follow (Phil. 4:9). **Am I spending time with a person I admire?**

Opportunity #4—Learn from Your Mistakes (John 8:11). **What recent mistakes have I made that caused me to change?**

Opportunity #5—Expose Yourself to Successful Experiences (Luke 11:1). **What positive event or person will I see today?**

III. The God Above You

Strength #1—God's Word (2 Tim. 3:16-17). **Am I receiving daily strength from God's Word?**

Strength #2—Prayer (James 5:16). **Am I praying daily and specifically about my attitude?**

Strength #3—The Holy Spirit (1 John 4:4). **Am I continually being filled with the Holy Spirit?**

Notes

CHAPTER TWO

1. John H. Sammis, "Trust and Obey," composed by Danial Brink Towner, 1887.

CHAPTER THREE

1. J. Sidlow Baxter, *Awake, My Heart* (Grand Rapids, Michigan: Zondervan Publishing House, 1960), 10.

CHAPTER SIX

1. Tim LaHaye, *Spirit Controlled Temperment* rev. ed. (Carol Stream, IL: Tyndale House Publishers, 1994).

CHAPTER SEVEN

1. Edgar A. Guest, "It Couldn't Be Done," accessed December 4, 2013, http://www.poetryfoundation.org/poem/173579.

CHAPTER EIGHT

1. Judith Viorst, *Alexander and the Terrible, Horrible, No Good, Very Bad Day* (New York: Atheneum Publishers, 1976).

CHAPTER NINE

1. The Church of Christ at Sycamore Chapel, Ashland City, Tennessee, May 24, 1998 Bulletin, page 3.
2. Harold Sherman, *How to Turn Failure into Success* (Upper Saddle River, New Jersey: Prentice Hall, 1958).

CHAPTER TEN

1. The Christophers, *Better to Light One Candle* (New York: Continuum, 1999).

CHAPTER THIRTEEN

1. Mitch Anthony, *Your Clients for Life* (Chicago, Illinois: Dearborn, 2002), 1.

CHAPTER FOURTEEN

1. Richard Foster, *Celebration of Discipline*, 3rd ed. (San Francisco, California: Harper Collins, 2002).

STUDY GUIDE

✧✧

CHAPTER 1

It's a Bird . . .
It's a Plane . . .
No, It's an Attitude!

1. Imagine you are the pilot in the cockpit of an airplane. Go ahead, you can do it! So you are flying along . . . What would you keep your eye on to monitor the performance of the airplane? How could you control its performance?

2. Now imagine yourself seated in the cockpit of your life. What is the critical factor in determining your spiritual, mental, and physical performance, no matter what kind of "weather" you encounter?

3. Rate yourself by the standard of attitude ascribed to Jesus by the apostle Paul. Give yourself a five if you feel really good about yourself on this particular attitude.

a. I am selfless.

☐ 0   ☐ 1   ☐ 2   ☐ 3   ☐ 4   ☐ 5

b. I am secure.

☐ 0   ☐ 1   ☐ 2   ☐ 3   ☐ 4   ☐ 5

c. I am submissive.

☐ 0   ☐ 1   ☐ 2   ☐ 3   ☐ 4   ☐ 5

Now, if you want to know how others view you, have your spouse or a close friend rate you.

4. According to Romans 12:1–2, what needs to happen if our attitude is to reflect God's will for us?

5. Tackle just one life situation that may be giving you fits, one that is clearly affecting your attitude. Apply King David's threefold process of praise. Describe the process as it applies to your life situation.

a. Praise begins with the will (Ps. 34:1).
b. Praise flows to the emotions (Ps. 34:2).
c. Praise spreads to others (Ps. 34:2–3).

6. Take the attitude indicator test.

Never been better	☐ *Yes*	☐ *No*
Never been worse	☐ *Yes*	☐ *No*
Nose-high	☐ *Yes*	☐ *No*
Nose-down	☐ *Yes*	☐ *No*

CHAPTER 2

The Attitude—What Is It?

1. Consider a time when you had

   - a positive attitude.
   - a problem attitude.

   Assess the impact on your family, church, work, and environment. This is not to be a judgmental exercise, but an attempt to assess the impact of attitudes.

2. "That's just my personality," you say. How does personality type affect attitudes toward others? Toward life situations?

3. How do facial expressions and body language affect others in a group? How do they affect the speaker?

4. What does your predominant facial expression and body language communicate at home? On the job? In social situations?

5. What is the connection between obedience to Christ and our attitude?

6. In what situations can we learn to trust the Lord through obedience? Use the example of the wedding at Cana.

7. In what way is your attitude the "librarian of your past"?

CHAPTER 3

The Attitude—Why Is It Important?

1. If you have been getting negative feedback from people, what may that indicate about you?

2. Though it should be obvious, what is the primary force that will determine whether we succeed or fail?

3. Circle your response to the question, "How do you feel the world is treating you?"

   a. Terrible.
   b. Just so-so.
   c. Pretty average.
   d. Really excellent.

4. If your answer is "terrible" or "so-so," would you agree or disagree with the author's statement, "Sometimes the prison of discontent has been built by our own hands"? If you disagree, why?

5. What can we learn from the apostle Paul's statements in Philippians 3:13–14? How can we apply them in our lives?

6. Since we cannot tailor most life situations to fit our desires, what can we do about them? Over what do we have control?

7. What are some of the frustrating, annoying, down-right horrible experiences you are having with others that make a positive attitude appear impossible?

a. At home:
b. On the road:
c. At work:
d. At church:

8. What role does having a positive attitude in those situations play in making you a loved and successful person?

9. Select the person with whom you are having the greatest difficulty, and for one week seek several opportunities to say positive, encouraging things to that person every day. Evaluate that person's attitude toward you after that week.

10. What gives many achievers that slight edge over their contemporaries, even though their peers may be smarter and better educated? Now describe someone in your family or circle of acquaintances who demonstrates the qualities you've just listed.

11. Maxims, or short truths, are like jewels that sparkle in many-faceted ways. Write down three maxims that caught your attention as you read the section under "Attitude Axiom #5."

1.
2.
3.

Now, put them on 3 x 5 cards, add the situation in your life to which each applies, and carry them with you so you can pull them out and let them inspire you anew. If you have access to a computer with graphics, make your own posters.

12. Do you know a "no limit" person in your family, church, community, or work? Analyze what gives that person an edge on others. It is not too late to become a "no limit" person yourself. Identify the limitation you have placed on yourself and draw from your observation how you could be released to become a "no limit" person.

13. Why doesn't being a Christian automatically give us a good attitude? If Christ is living in us through the Holy Spirit, who is responsible for our wrong attitudes?

CHAPTER 4

It's Hard to Soar with the Eagles When You Have to Live with the Turkeys

1. Victor Frankl asserted, "The last of the human freedoms is to choose one's attitude in *any* given set of circumstances." Do you agree or disagree? Why or why not? Can you give an example?

2. After reading the story about the man with the negative upbringing, reflect on what attitude appears to have been passed from generation to generation in your family. What decision do you need to make?

3. Take time to fill in the Attitude Application Chart on page 33. Preferably retreat to your favorite "think it through" place, a special chair, a spot in the yard, a mountain park, or a beach. Pray that God will allow to surface those conditions that you need to recognize as formative, even destructive, and the choices that resulted.

CHAPTER 5

Foundational Truths About the Construction of the Attitude

1. What attitudes did you pick up in childhood that still threaten to derail efforts to improve your attitude? If you experienced a childhood with positive attitudes, what elements of that input are providing the "engine" for positive change?

2. What attitude growth, whether positive or negative, do you detect in yourself? In your spouse?

3. The very fact that you have been reading this book and are working through this study guide provides positive reinforcement of good attitudes. But as part of that reinforcement, record which of your attitudes specifically need deepening and reinforcing. List one step you can take right now to do it.

4. Rather than concentrating on negative input, ask God to help you find positive reinforcement from significant people in your life. And if at all possible, send at least one of those people a thank-you card this week.

CHAPTER 6

Materials That Are Used in Constructing an Attitude

1. If you completed the Attitude Application review on pages 40–42, reexamine what you wrote in light of the answers you have given in this study guide. The lapse of time, the stifling of memories, may mean you'll want to change some answers you gave earlier.

2. Have you identified which of the four temperaments is most likely yours? If so, which of the descriptive phrases most accurately describes your attitude?

3. Each of us lives a part of our lives in an environment that is negative. For some, home life means constantly battling a spouse's negative attitudes. For others, it may be the office, or a specific customer who rubs them the wrong way. Even a long commute can generate increasingly negative attitudes. Describe the most negative environment in your life—and keep it in mind as you work through this book.

4. You've read the author's experiences of adult affirmation. What are yours? Thank God for them! Identify where and how you can provide that kind of affirmation—and write down your response as confirmation of that desire.

5. The author clearly has a positive self-image. He mentions several keys to feeling good about oneself. Highlight them in the text and write them out to fix them in your mind.

6. Notice how the author felt good about helping his daughter succeed. Whom can you help succeed? Write down a plan of action, even though it may be incomplete.

7. The author writes, "We always have a number of opportunities in our hands. We must decide whether to take a risk and act on them" (page 48). What are the opportunities in your life that will demand taking a risk?

8. A leading pastor who experienced an emotional crisis discovered that he had only one friend who provided uplifting, growth-oriented input, more than two dozen who drained him, and several who were neutral. When he returned to active ministry, he determined to significantly increase the number of friends who were self-assured enough to provide positive input. What kind of input do your peers provide? Do you need to seek different peer relationships?

9. Our home environment and the attitudes of our spouses and children may provide the most negative input we get. If so, what positive steps can we take to overcome that?

- See a pastor or counselor.
- Enter into a prayer pact with a close friend.
- Begin a deliberate campaign to provide positive input to your spouse.
- Lovingly, and in a neutral location (restaurant, park, beach), confront the guilty party.

CHAPTER 7

The Costliest Mistake People Make in Constructing an Attitude

1. What was the label that, upon reflection, proved to be either the most limiting, or provided the greatest challenge for you when trying to break through the sap barrier?

2. In what areas of your life are you failing to exceed the sap strata line:

   - in terms of physical exertion?
   - in terms of a spiritual discipline?
   - in terms of family experiences?
   - in terms of job risk-taking?

   Now, set a goal in one area that will help you exceed the sap strata line.

3. Describe one experience that proved so painful that you have never ventured to repeat it. Now analyze how you could break through the pain barrier in a similar event in the future.

CHAPTER 8

Mayday! Mayday! My Attitude Is Losing Altitude

1. What are three things the author encourages the reader to remember "when the going gets tough"?

   1.
   2.
   3.

2. Any rough weather? What key thought can keep you going, according to Galatians 6:9?

3. What is our "second wind" in serving the Lord according to Hebrews 12:1–3?

4. Do you face a potential squall in your home life or on the job? What can you do to avoid it? Apply the following criteria:

   a. Do I lack the experience necessary to weather this storm?
   b. Do I lack the knowledge to navigate through the storm?
   c. Do I lack the time to make necessary preparations?
   d. Do I lack facts to make a proper decision?
   e. Do I lack sufficient prayer to weather the storm?

5. How can we know if we are not in touch with the "control tower"?

6. "What really matters is what happens in us, not to us." Do you agree or disagree? Why or why not?

CHAPTER 9

The Crash from Within

1. The author's list of major failures by people we now consider heroes reminds us that failure need not be fatal.

   a. Describe an experience of failure in your life that you thought would destroy you, but it didn't.
   b. Describe an experience of failure that proved, in retrospect, to be a stepping-stone.

2. If you are truly honest with yourself, how is fear of failure in a specific area preventing you from making progress?

3. Comment on the author's statement, "Accepting failure in the positive sense becomes effective when you believe that the right to fail is as important as the right to succeed" (page 68).

4. What implication does the following statement have for you: "Until we accept the fact that the future of the world does not hinge on our decisions, we will be unable to forget past mistakes. Attitude is the determining factor of whether our failures make us or break us" (page 69).

5. How does John 12:24–25 relate to the whole issue of fear of failure?

6. What are the four things that discouragement does to us?

   1.
   2.
   3.
   4.

7. Consider a discouraging situation in your life. Now apply the four steps the author recommends, describing how they fit your situation.

   a. Positive Action:
   b. Positive Thinking:
   c. Positive Example:
   d. Positive Persistence:

8. How do you relate to the apostle Paul's struggle as described in Romans 7:15–25? Don't be afraid to be real and honest.

CHAPTER 10

The Crash from Without

1. What would you consider the most traumatic, personally distressing criticism from someone close to you? If you are still smarting from this criticism, analyze whether it was justified, or a case of "the best fruit is the one the birds pick."

2. Now evaluate whether that particular criticism is, as in Jesus' case:

   • an opportunity to comfort.
   • an opportunity to heal.
   • an opportunity to overcome.
   • an opportunity to forgive.

3. What can we learn from Jesus' teaching in Matthew 5:43–48 regarding our response to criticism?

4. Name a friend who encourages you when criticism comes. Then name a person whose criticism is damaging.

5. What is the implication of Robert Louis Stevenson's comment, "I will never permit a row of medicine bottles to block my horizon" (page 83)? List three or four "medicine bottles" in your life that are threatening to keep your eyes off Jesus' presence and His provisions.

6. What is the "change" that is potentially a source of discomfort:

- in your home?
- in your church?
- on the job?
- in your community?

7. Examine that change and evaluate it in light of the author's comment, "With the proper attitude, all change, whether positive or negative, will be a learning experience that results in a growing experience" (page 84). What could be the learning component in that change? What could be the growth component?

8. In the U.S. today the media focuses almost exclusively on negative news. In what ways could this color your thinking about what God could do in the future? So you can bring them before the Lord in prayer and be renewed, list the typically negative thoughts that tend to dominate your life after or while watching the television news.

9. How does negative thinking limit our potential? If possible, respond in terms of a specific situation in your life at home, at church, in the community, or on the job.

10. What are some of the "Impossibles" you have achieved or seen others achieve?

CHAPTER 11

Up, Up, and Away

1. What is the good news for those imprisoned by their bad attitudes?

2. What excuses have you or someone you love been giving for bad attitudes?

3. Identify a friend who can pray with you and hold you accountable as you work toward changing a negative attitude.

CHAPTER 12

The Choice Within You

Ready for real change? This is the action chapter. However, if you have been conscientiously following the suggestions in the study guide, you will already be well underway. In this chapter we will focus on key areas, rather than on every step suggested by the author, even though we urge you to take every step in the process he provides.

1. Work through the Stages of Evaluation.

    a. Identify Problem Feelings:
    b. Identify Problem Behavior:
    c. Identify Problem Thinking:
    d. Identify Biblical Thinking:
    e. Secure Commitment:
    f. Plan and Carry Out Your Choice:

2. Identify the fear in your life. It may be fear of failure, fear of change, fear of criticism. If you are in a group, discuss the common fears that prevent change and illustrate them. After writing down these fears, initiate the Four-Step Formula to Handle Fear.

3. Highlight the negative words or phrases on page 105 that are most common to you. Now copy them as part of the process of eliminating them from your vocabulary.

4. What are the three times people are most receptive to change?

   1.
   2.
   3.

5. Is there a sin, a transgression, or an abuse that is like a chain, holding you to your past? As you read Psalm 51, underline the key truths that meant the most to you. Write out what action you plan to take.

6. Compare your thought patterns with Philippians 4:8. Write out the area that most needs attention if you are to change your thought pattern.

7. Which circle of habits best describes you? If you fit the "Bad Habits" progression, work through the steps on page 112 in terms of only one bad habit at a time.

8. If earlier in this series you identified a negative attitude and began the process of change, at what stage are you? (Refer to pages 112–113.) If at the Late Stage, describe how you will get back on track.

CHAPTER 13

The Opportunities Around You

1. Are the qualifications for a friend too idealistic? Can someone be a true friend without meeting every qualification suggested?

2. Why is the following observation true or false: "While counseling people facing a broken marriage, I have observed that often the couple's friends are also having marriage problems" (page 117)?

3. One of the more difficult steps for a person to take is to admit he needs a model, to identify that model, and to ask for discipling by that model. Yet amazing progress can be made by both men and women willing to submit to that discipline. If you are a young adult, do not be afraid to ask an older adult to meet with you regularly for discipling purposes—he or she will be glad to help. Write out the qualities you are looking for in a model who can assist you in changing a particular attitude.

4. Identify a recent experience of failure. Now draw on the example of the boy who lost a hand (page 120), evaluating what you have left that is positive.

5. How can we expose ourselves to successful experiences? Do not limit yourself to your immediate circle of friends! A pastor taking on a new assignment in a large inner-city church visited five pastors heading up large, successful city churches. He spent a weekend

with each before beginning his new ministry and attempted to learn from each one's success. No wonder he learned and changed. So pick your "winners," list them, and then deliberately expose yourself to their successful experiences.

CHAPTER 14

The God Above You

1. Why do we limit God as we consider change in our lives?

2. Describe your personal feelings as you read the two "Foundation" statements. Have you been able to say them without feelings of doubt?

3. Summarize for yourself why you should be able to say the following confidently:

   a. "I am truly significant."
   b. "I am truly secure."

4. The author provides reassuring Scripture passages, but of even greater value are those you discover for yourself. Using a concordance, look up the word *power* in the letters of Paul. Highlight those verses in your Bible. Copy them on 3 x 5 cards to remind you of Christ's power available to you.

5. If prayer is so important to change, what does it do for you that is truly unique?

6. How can we acquire the power of the Holy Spirit, since He is the true Change Agent?

About the Author

John C. Maxwell is an internationally renowned leadership expert, coach, and author with more than 22 million books sold. Dr. Maxwell founded the John Maxwell Company, John Maxwell Team, and EQUIP, organizations that have trained more than 5 million leaders in 185 countries. Every year he speaks to Fortune 500 and 100 companies, international government leaders, and organizations such as the United States Military Academy at West Point, the NFL, and the United Nations. A *New York Times*, *Wall Street Journal*, and *Business Week* best-selling author, Maxwell's *The 21 Irrefutable Laws of Leadership* has sold more than 2 million copies. *Developing the Leader Within You* and *The 21 Indispensable Qualities of a Leader* have each sold more than 1 million copies. You can follow him on Twitter @ JohnCMaxwell and read his blog at JohnMaxwell.com.

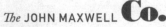